An Italian Fellowship Journey

Civita Veritas

GABRIELA DENISE FRANK

Civita Veritas: An Italian Fellowship Journey
Title ID: 3529928
ISBN-13: 978-1456536206

Cover Photograph © Perri Lynch
Author Photograph © Lonnie Tristan Renteria
Interior Photography and Art © Gabriela Denise Frank

Map of Civita di Bagnoregio Courtesy of
The Northwest Institute for Architecture and Urban Studies in Italy (NIAUSI)

To the exquisite women who have nurtured and inspired me throughout my life — and to Astra, whose legacy gave me something to reach for.

Prologue

Before I began this fellowship journey, I did not realize how challenging it is to tell "the truth," especially when writing a piece of non-fiction. When we read someone else's writing, we volunteer to take on her perspective, along with its observations, agendas—and blind spots. As I received feedback on my work, especially from those who have known Civita longer than I have, I was reminded that there is not one truth, but many.

Describing my experience was like trying to reconstruct a broken mirror—I discovered that what I pieced together formed a prism rather than a single reflection. Each facet of is true…from a certain perspective.

This book is not intended to stand as a definitive portrait of Civita di Bagnoregio or a biography of its residents. Others have recorded exhaustive technical analyses about Civita's built form and history—and related volumes are in the works through the Northwest Institute for Architecture and Urban Studies in Italy (NIAUSI), the organization that sponsored my fellowship.

As a writer, I sought to create something wholly distinct: a personal, emotional bridge between Civita and the outside world, told as if my readers and I were sitting in conversation with one another. Most of this material originally appeared as daily blog entries during the summer of 2010. While on site, I approached my work as a personal investigation of place—a story equally intended to explore and explain the material world as much as invoke a spiritual journey experienced through my words.

The comment I heard most often from those who followed my posts was, "I felt like I was right there with you." In composing these essays, I retained a first-person account because only a personal narrative could convey the intimacy and exposure that I sought to communicate.

For instance, one morning in late September, I bounded out of bed, knowing that it was the right day to write about the sunrise. As luck would have it, that morning held the last clear dawn for the duration of my stay. Why did I wait? Where did the faith come from that the right moment would present itself? How did I know it when it arrived?

The short answer is, magic. How else could I recreate the magic that I felt in each discovery, but in the first person?

This leads to another note on my endeavor: throughout my journey, I exercised a purposeful absence of a strict writing plan or narrative structure. It never felt right to do more than create a broad list of topics that I hoped to cover as I became inspired, such as time, language, seasons, building forms, public spaces, religion, food, gardens, etc. Ultimately, this was the right choice.

The personal transformation that blooms in Civita is inexplicable; it doesn't happen to everyone who stays there, but it is common amongst those who arrive seeking it. I also learned to take things bit by bit *(piano, piano)*—everything has its right time. I couldn't give words to it then, but I see now that I could not have truly appreciated the sunrise if it was the first thing I had encountered. Only after delving into storms and exploring gardens in the night did I have any real appreciation for the power of dawn.

Likewise, only after the adventure was over could I look back with any perspective to know in what order to present these stories to showcase the experience in the most powerful light.

With that, I invite you to join this journey as I began it: by leaving behind any notion of Civita as a dying city. Instead, peer through my eyes to find a different world:

…you will reside in an old stone house and speak Italian without a dictionary;

…you will kiss people on the cheeks when you meet and depart;

…you will drink young red wine from the valley and make dinner from the garden; and

…you will watch time stretch out like warm taffy as you bathe in the most yellow of sunlight.

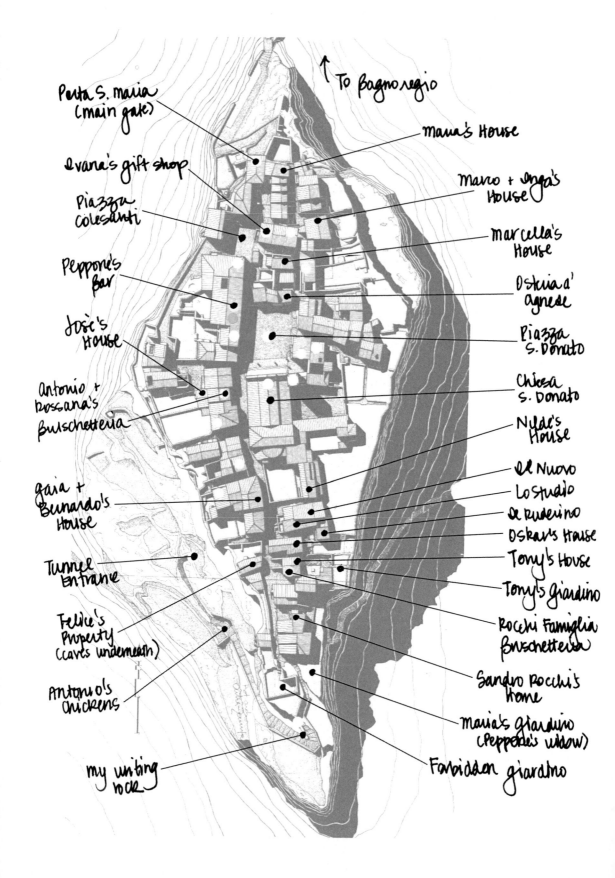

Perta S. maria
(main gate)

Ivana's gift shop

Piazza
Colesanti

Peppone's
Bar

Josie's
House

Antonio +
Rossana's
Bruschetteria

Gaia +
Bernardo's
House

Tunnel
Entrance

Felice's
Property
(caves underneath)

Antonio's
Chickens

my writing
rock

To Bagno regio

Maria's House

Marco + Inga's
House

Marcella's
House

Osteria a'
agnese

Piazza
S. Donato

Chiesa
S. Donato

Nilde's
House

Il Nuovo

Lo Studio

Il Ruderino

Oskar's House

Tony's House

Tony's giardino

Rocchi Famiglia
Bruschetteria

Sandro Rocchi's
Home

Maria's giardino
(Peppone's widow)

Forbidden giardino

Cast of Characters

Alessio
A young shoe designer from northern Italy who owns a home in Civita.

Antonio and Rossana
Rossana, the daughter of Domenica and Mario (both deceased), is married to Antonio; together, they run a *bruschetteria con prodotti locali* in Civita over which they own a home. They have two beautiful blond daughters, Antonella and Arianna. During my stay, they invited me to the baptism of their grand daughter, Elena.

Always quick with a wave and a smile, Antonio can often be found firing bread or slicing ingredients for my favorite menu items: *bruschetta con carciofi* (grilled bread with artichokes), *verdure mista grigliata* (mixed grilled vegetables), and *salsiccia di maiale* (pork sausage). Rossana can be seen managing the floor to keep the flow of service moving efficiently.

Civita di Bagnoregio
Located approximately 60 miles north of Rome in Italy's central province of Lazio, Civita di Bagnoregio is an ancient hill town set within a remarkable geological landscape. With Etruscan underpinnings, Civita's first inhabitation predates the founding of Rome. Because the historic citadel does not provide for automobile access, this hilltown has retained an unusually intact community of buildings, spaces and ambience dating largely from medieval and Renaissance times.

Emanuela and Raphaele
Emanuela and Raphaele own the Osteria al Forno d'Agnese in Civita named after his grandmother. We dined several times on their patio, enjoying fried *fiori di zucca* (zucchini flowers), *gnocchi con pomodoro e basilico* (potato dumplings with tomato and basil), and *stracceti con rucola e pinoli* (beef with arugula and pine nuts). The couple live in Bagnoregio with their 7-year-old son.

Familigia Rocchi
Children of Vittoria and Luigi (deceased), the family is helmed by two brothers, Sandro and Felice, who co-own the temporarily closed Antico Frantoio Bruschetteria. Sandro's children are Alessandra, an architect, and Mauritzio, a security officer at Fiumincino airport. Felice's children are Cinzia, whom I did not meet, and Fabrizio, who owns an *agriturismo* in the valley below Civita (*http://www.corone-civita.com/it/index.html*). Alessandra has two boys, Giovanni and Ludivico; Fabrizio has a daughter, Chiara.

Both Sandro and Fabrizio produce local wine and olive oil; Felice and his wife own a building with Etruscan tools and an olive press that is open daily for viewing.

Famiglia Rossi Doria
Bernardo and Gaia Rossi Doria own a home *vicino* Tony's house, facing onto the *decumanus maximus*. Bernardo was an architect and university professor prior to his retirement; Gaia was a teacher. I learned late in my stay that Bernardo also served as Deputy Mayor of Rome for a time; he was asked to provide counsel to the Vatican during his tenure.

When I met them, Bernardo was on crutches after being struck—and nearly killed—in April by a car in Rome. With white hair that underlines his scholarly demeanor, Bernardo speaks Italian with a soft accent, as his first language is actually French. Gaia, who comes from the south of Italy, is a wiry goddess with dark curly hair and copper highlights from the sun. They have two daughters, Ilaria and Priscilla.

A landscape architect, Ilaria is Gaia and Bernardo's older daughter who lives in Rome and shares a life with Marco De Petrillo, a partner in a travel firm called Viaggi in Avventura (VIA.) Priscilla is Ilaria's younger sister who lives in London with her husband and two children, Emma and Thomas.

Father Marco
Soft-spoken and gentle, Father Marco lives in a monastery in Bagnoregio, but specifically ministers to the parish in Civita. Tall, thin, and likely in his 40s, Father Marco sports closely shorn gray hair and wire frame glasses. He is often seen climbing the bridge to Civita wearing his black backpack, on his way to prepare the *chiesa* for services.

Gabriele and Ciro
Together, Gabriele Di Giandomenico and Ciro Cristiano own the Trattoria dell'Orso on Via della Misericordia in Orvieto. They make a supreme guinea fowl with truffle sauce.

Gatti (Cats)
Tony's house is cradle to six cats: Nerone, the head cat (*capo gatto*), who is black with a brown sheen and yellow eyes; Figaro, who wears a tuxedo; Betty, a tabby cat; Shaw, a white calico; and Massimo, a black cat with a large head—and possibly the father of Betty's *gattino, Due Mila Dieci* (2010.)

Helen
On sabbatical for a year as she contemplated her future, Helen came to Civita during a two-month European adventure. A Seattle resident, Helen and I discovered that we shared many similar experiences, including a disastrous undertaking of Leslie Mackey's Harvest Pie for Thanksgiving dessert last year—which took both of us 11 hours to cook, as we each slaved until nearly midnight. If only we had known each other then.

Iole
Hailing from Abruzzo, Iole Alessandrini is an architect and artist who grew up in Rome. Years later, in a twist of fate, she met Astra there through a design contest. With encouragement from Astra, Iole moved to Seattle 16 years ago and currently lives in Astra and Tony's home near the University of Washington. An accomplished artist, Iole also teaches courses through the UW in Venice and Rome.

Ivana
Ivana owns the gift shop facing onto Civita's Piazza Colesanti. A petite brunette, we would often meet when she was out for a stroll or coming up from Bagnoregio. She also owns the home above her gift shop.

Jerry and Ron
Brothers Jerry and Ron stayed in Tony's garden house when they visited Civita just after Sue, Kirstin, and Helen left. Jerry, who lives in Seattle, has visited Civita for over 25 years; his daughter was baptized in the church. His younger brother, Ron, is a photographer who lives in Northern California.

Jonathan

Jonathan is a recent University of Washington architectural school graduate who currently resides in Idaho. One of the first NIAUSI interns, collectively called The Gang of Four, Jonathan spent several weeks cataloguing the library in Civita over the summer of 2010.

Josè

Josè, whose full name is Giuseppina d'Amely-Melodia, is a graduate of Harvard and a longtime friend of Astra and Tony's. Coincidentally, she shared an oceanliner with Astra on her return to Italy after college, though the two formally met through an architect named Malcom Davis.

A stately, stylish woman who speaks several languages, Josè worked for Italy's Finance and Fiscal Department during her career. She currently lives in Rome and owns a home Civita, the first of Astra's renovations, which is located on the other side of Antonio and Rossana's *bruschetteria*.

Laura

Hailing from the valley below Civita, Laura is married to Roberto; their son, Alberto, was baptized in the church in Civita. Kind and friendly, Laura cleans and maintains the NIAUSI properties and Tony's home.

Luca

An artist and, until recently, a home owner in Civita, Luca de Troia now resides in a garden retreat of his own making called Hortus Unicorni (*http://www.hortusunicorni.com*), about 20 minutes away. Over the past 15 years, he has imported, planted and nurtured countless plant species from around the world in this little Eden. He restored the *ruderino* on site into a grand manor where he now lives with his dog, Ito.

Mancini Sisters

Anna Rita (Anna Ri) and Gentillina (Gentilli) own the *alimentari* where I bought meat, cheese and general foodstuffs. Both blondes by choice, Gentilli is the older sister who often works the register while AnnaRi slices the finest *prosciutto* and *primo sale* (buffalo mozzarella with only the "first salt"). Whenever I shopped with them, they greeted me with, *"Ciao, cara."*

Marco and Inga

Both anesthesiologists, Marco and Inga own a home on the western edge of Civita. This summer, they visited with their two children: Nina, who is close to graduating from college, and Niko, who is about to begin. Marco is Italian and quite tall, likely in his early 50s with curly brown hair, while Inga is Eastern European and petite. Both children are striking, lanky blonds.

Maria *di Giardino*

Elderly Maria, an institution in Civita, sits outside a garden and charges admission to those who take a view. Turns out, the garden is not even hers. The victim of polio as a child, she is often seen seated as one foot is lame, the result of the disease. Her son, Sandro, is in his 50s; he comes to check in on Maria daily on his choppy *motorino*. Maria is the widow of Peppone, after whom is named the bar facing the main *piazza*.

Maria Grazia

With fawny brown hair and wire rim glasses, Maria Grazia is the warm vegetable shop owner in Bagnoregio who believes in exact change. If you ask, she will pull a bit of *prezzemolo* (parsley) for free from the back.

Maria *di Venezia* and Marcella

Maria, with jet-black hair, and Marcella, a bubbly blond, are two fabulous women who I met through Josè; they own homes in Civita that they visit in the summer.

Nilde

Nilde and her husband lived in the home that my kitchen window looked out at. A short, no-nonsense but kind woman with gray hair and red glasses, Nilde and I formally met at a dinner on Emanuela and Raphaele's patio. Due to age and issues with accessibility, Nilde and her husband sold their home and moved to Bagnoregio during my last days in Civita.

Oskar

Oskar owns the home across from Lo Studio, just on the other side of Tony's house. During Astra's renovation of his home, they discovered centuries-old frescoes under the stucco. Oskar also owns the garden on the other side of Tony's *giardino*.

Sandro

Sandro, or as Tony affectionately distinguishes him, Sandro Tractor Man, is employed by the Commune di Bagnoregio to transport goods to businesses in Civita with his small, red flatbed tractor. Occasionally, he gives luggage, groceries—and Tony—a lift.

Sue and Kirstin

Also known as my "out-laws," Sue and Kirstin are close friends who visited me in Civita; we've shared lives—and tables—for nearly 15 years. Sue and her husband, Tom, a former Delta pilot, live in Vancouver, Washington, while Kirstin recently relocated from San Francisco to Florida to join her partner, Scott.

Tony and Astra

Anthony Costa Heywood, who goes by Tony, is the surviving husband of the recently deceased Astra Zarina, a distinguished University of Washington professor who rediscovered Civita in the 1960s. During her initial visit, which included a tour of the *ruderino* (ruin or rustic home) that she felt compelled to purchase on first sight, Astra made it her personal mission to study and restore Civita. Tony and Astra were among the original founders of the Northwest Institute for Architecture and Urban Studies in Italy (NIAUSI.)

As an architect, Tony has lived and worked in Europe since the 1960s. For decades, he and Astra called Rome their primary residence and work, including the creation of the UW Rome Center and the extensive interventions of Palazzo Pio adjoining Campo dei' Fiori as the seat of UW programs in Italy. Tony and Astra eventually moved to Civita as their primary residence. Astra passed away in 2006; Tony continues to reside in Civita year-round.

He and Astra designed and renovated their own home, as well as the NIAUSI properties and several spaces in Civita. He considers the design of his garden pergola as his greatest achievement.

One

"When a place is billed as a dying city, people treat it as if there are no sacred spaces—everything is a quaint backdrop."

11 Agosto: The Journey Here

No ticket, no worries—there's counter help to check my 47-pound bag, just under limit. Musta-chioed Italian *nonna* brushes past me in her kerchief; I'm a specter she refuses to see. An American, one of millions, like harmless bees. *Vai, vai.* If she can jettison seven pounds from her hard-top luggage, she is flying home where I'm merely a visitor.

Bad teriyaki on S Concourse—no worse than chicken picatta on the plane with green beans boiled so no taste remains. Rowdy chums swear with Heineken-laced breath; the captain storms from the cockpit after one a.m. to set them straight. Hulking, soft-spoken Spaniard overflows into my seat while two tow-headed twins endlessly chatter and bleat. We shoot looks at their parents who don't quell their excitement; after all, none of us is really sleeping, anyway.

Amsterdam's Schipol at 8 a.m., familiar and orderly, directing me in yellow-orange Dutch signs that I can almost read. *"Ciao, principessa,"* he croons into his phone. Pegged jeans, yellow and blue sneakers, Armani glasses tucked into his shirt. I can picture her: a mane of wavy chestnut hair, legs up to here, and pouty red lips.

Or, perhaps, that mustachioed woman in Seattle.

I choose a train from Fiumincino to Rome over a white-knuckled taxi ride. *A Roma Termini prendo un espresso sorbetto,* my first purchase from which is born the 80 *centesimi* I need for the public toilet.

Time's on my side, but infernal train schedules never speak the truth! *Devo aiuto,* I beg a woman in an official-looking hat. She's sighing *vai, vai* in her mind as she points to my car and seat number on the ticket. Seven cars down, the train's chugging to depart! I mutter, *"Aspetta!"* to the conductor and, *"Vai!"* to myself, willing my legs to hurry. With Titan strength, I thrust my bag six feet in the air and pull myself up into *Carrozza* 2 in the nick of time.

Sweat-bursting brows, I find a cabin for six containing *il mio posto,* an Italian man and his son, and a Brazilian couple expecting a child. The son hoists my bag with a gallant sweep while I collapse in an exhausted heap. Chit-chat about dinner (what else?) as the father phones home, *maiale con pomodoro;* take me with you!

Their Italian flows over me in waves; meekly, I ask, *"Siamo vicino a Orvieto?"* and thus enter the conversation. Why am I in Italy? For how long? Is this my first visit? Will there be someone to pick me up *alla stazione?* The young Brazilian mother-to-be chides the old man for how quickly he speaks to me, while she praises my ability to understand.

"I could accompany you, if you need to find a ride," the son offers in richly accented English; a momentary temptation, but I assure him that I'm being met. I disembark alone, and there is Tony—tall, gray and waiting: we know each other instantly.

More gallantry, Tony takes my bag and shepherds me *nella macchina* down twisty, turning roads to Bagnoregio, which is everything that a small Italian town should be: a statue here, a *fontana* there, *l'ufficio postale,* and a vegetable shop. We dodge a head-on collision as a tiny white car takes a wide hairpin turn, arriving windswept but alive at Civita.

Vai, vai. He instructs me to seek out my new home while he graciously arranges for a truck to take my bag. On the narrow bridge, I don't look down. Vaguely, side to side, I sense the *belvedere.* It feels like climbing Seattle's Queen Anne hill until the very last bit, that steep incline and then the turn. Up, up, up to find sweet intern, Jonathan, in the Ruderino. We fall instantly into Civita Speak, that enthusiastic, effervescent conversation about daily life here.

Rest, repose and unpack. Buzz-buzz, the quiet hum of bugs. Salt-laced skin thirsty for a wash. A sweet peach sates the gnaw in my belly with local Lazio juices flowing freely over my chin. Coaxing clothes from my bag, whose guts spill out on the bed, I'm tempted to stay for a catnap.

The bell tolls eight, time for *la cena con* Tony, Jonathan *e il gatto,* Massimo. *Naturalmente, beviamo vino rosso* under a grapevine arbor as evening approaches. *Prosciutto e melone* followed by *risotto al forno* with ham, parsley, celery, and cucumber.

I eat three helpings.

An opera sings tinnily on Tony's radio as we eat and drink, telling stories. *Vai, vai,* we lazily shoo the evening insects away.

Lubriano lights beam from across the way. Growing dark calls the stars out to play. Night winds carry band music from the valley below. Gelato and nips of brandy accompany rustling vines that sing along with gentle *piazza* sounds, echoing on stone walls.

Quieter, quieter the evening grows; nine, ten o'clock. A distracted wasp falls in love with the light, breaking up our little party with his insistent banging.

After 30 hours awake, I cannot resist my bed. My eyes drift to my notebook, but the pillow's call is stronger. A voice suggests attempting to capture the day, but I muster, *"Vai, vai,"* until it goes away.

A City in Expectation

A hushed stage reset: Raphele sprays the *piazza* down wet as the hazy miasma floats north and west. Even insects take rest, as I can attest—they've stopped feasting freely on my arms and my legs.

Dishes clank as they're stacked, glasses clink in the rack, and silverware clangs as it's cleaned by disinterested bar maids. Punctuating the din, the silence of wiping and then—**kaboom**—a pounding abounding from the Trattoria Antico Forno.

As if on cue, a young priest crosses in view, navigating the *piazza* soundlessly in his high-collared frock. Services or festival, who knows? Inside he goes, his robes billow behind him, black like a cloud. Friday at three, only the *piazza* and me, writing notes from my perch on the bench.

Waitresses emerge, cell phones in hand, *loro fumano le sigarette* while they talk with their hands. *Chiacchierrare*—or chit-chat, as we say—they slink into the shade and lean up against walls with long gamine frames. Delicate puffs escape their fast-moving lips; in *moda bella* they appear irritated yet bored, hands set on hips.

With a huff and a click, the calls end in a tiff—and so, too, concludes the first act of the day.

Act Two begins as clouds roll past again, signaling our cast that their afternoon audience is here. As the sun emerges, so do the tourists, heralded by—scratch, scratch—the grinding of sandals on stones. A corpulent herd, they waddle through town; a man caresses his belly and a dull roar abounds as terrible *bambini* burst into the square.

Crowds of locusts descend: *sposati* and friends, they pour in like lava in irrepressible waves. They slurp from the fountain hose like field animals at troughs—how uncivilized this *acqua minerale*! I'd offer a glass, but my guess is they'd pass; after all, *qual è la differenza?*

The priest, sensing his cue, abandons his pew and emerges on the *piazza's* quickly drying dirt stage. His hand finds his cross—a wooden albatross—he tugs hard to unloosen it, like it's too heavy to bear. He pretends not to see the tourists or me, so intent on his path out of Civita's square.

Basta! (Enough!) With that I give up, too many people snap-snapping photos of this house and that. A kiss to Alessandra and *"Salve!"* to Bernardo; they move through the *piazza* without stopping to rest. What takes place in Act Three we likely won't see, though the smell of the fires gives us a hint.

Each day the *piazza* expects such shows: mad morning rush and afternoon tours. *Secondo me,* the quiet moments of preparation in between speak best to the soul that's held here. Cleaning dishes by hand, watering patios and sand, and smelling the breeze as it elevates the aroma of bread. With slight sounds from their feet, Civitonici step through the streets, lithe and invisible like cats amused by this divine comedy.

17 Agosto: Strangers and Famiglia

Before the left turn off of Via Mercatello, Civita's main street, brings you to the courtyard beneath my home, Il Nuovo, there are brown double-doors leading into a stone building on the right. Each day, I peer through the door, which always stands ajar, to find a sawhorse blocking the corridor.

Last night, Ilaria, part of the family who resides there, found Tony and me in the garden just after 19:00 *ore*. Tony was gathering basil to make fried eggplant while I petted the head cat, Nerone, as he writhed precariously, if not defiantly, in a sunny spot on the high wall. He didn't seem concerned that a 300-foot drop to the valley floor stood mere inches away.

Ilaria invited us on behalf of her parents, Gaia and Bernardo, to their home for dinner. We agreed to bring our *melanzane*, the first of several ventures gone awry in the past 24 hours. After growing confident in cooking with Tony, I should have known it was time for a stumble.

First, I chopped the eggplant too thick, then I tried slicing what I had in half after his admonition ("Those are too big; make them look like the picture," he said.) When we boiled them, most of the pieces disintegrated into thin, ropy slop.

The best slices fried alright, so I inventively combined a few together in the mixture of egg, cheese, basil, and garlic before popping them into the sunflower oil. The result was a bubbling explosion of hot oil onto the stovetop, as if from a high school science project.

At this point, I quit attempting to help and begged forgiveness, knowing that our offering would be meager. So much for *la vita bella italiana*, I thought, my heart sinking.

We arrived after 20:00 *ore* with a small dish of acceptable *melanzane fritte*, moving aside the sawhorse (meant for discouraging the curious tourist hordes) in order to ascend the stairs. We entered a warmly apportioned old-world home with a massive hearth, 20-foot ceilings, and a grand wooden dining table set for six. Emma and Thomas, children of Gaia and Bernardo's visiting daughter, Priscilla, were already asleep downstairs.

In spite of needing crutches to walk, white-haired Bernardo, whose skin is light like mine, served us wine and invited us to sit with him at the table. The women swept in and out, bringing food and water, beginning with an appetizer of salted caper blossom pods and *prosciutto* in olive oil.

In contemplating the women, I immediately fell in love with their intelligence, easy confidence, and unadorned beauty. Southern blooded, Gaia's deep brown skin wraps tightly around her long, lanky limbs. Her slender face and sparkling eyes are topped by outrageously curly short brown hair touched with natural copper highlights. Both daughters inherited her looks, though older daughter Ilaria's hair is not quite as curly or dark, and Priscilla wears her solid espresso brown locks in shoulder-length waves.

Even after a week in Civita, I felt lost in their rapid dinner conversation. They spoke quickly about complex topics such as Berlusconi, politics, the day's news, and work matters. In addition to their speed, their vocabulary was beyond me. I felt dismayed and exhausted, spacing out on simple sentence construction and correct conjugation, though they helped to correct me.

After our initial course of *pasta fagiole* followed by *insalata con patate, pomodori e olive*—and our *melan-zane*, which they kindly assured us was delicious—I finally fell into English. Thankfully, they did the same so that I could converse with a little less effort. They commented on the rush of tourists in town on holiday, an overwhelming number.

"Today, I heard them outside," Gaia said, personifying their ignorance, "*'See those windows? I think someone's in there; it must be one of the seven residents.'* Seven residents?! If that were true, it would be this whole room!"

A general disdain is held for those who intrude on the peace and quiet of Civita, as if it's Euro-Disney. After a week, even I feel annoyed by the tourists' loud speech, constant photography, and irreverent picnicking in my courtyard. Fueled by travel guides, visitors treat Civita like a ghost town with abandoned buildings for them to probe without respect or restraint.

As we enjoyed fresh fruit and ricotta cheese for dessert, I was able to contribute my small irritation to the conversation, explaining how *i touristi* commonly climb my stairs and attempt to enter my home while I'm working.

Gaia nodded knowingly, adding that it is quite trying for the families who summer in Civita. I smiled in agreement thinking that, perhaps my presence here is becoming a bit less strange after all.

19 Agosto: Fare il Portoghese

Today, I invite you to inhabit the body of a tourist.

You're staying in Bagnoregio and wish to lunch in charming Civita. Still digesting your breakfast of *cappuccino, cornetto* and yogurt, you leave your hotel in the warm late morning. Your wife pushes a stroller with your baby son inside while your three-year-old daughter skips around with wild energy that you once possessed.

Winding through town, you find the shady side of the streets, taking a shortcut by the café in the pine trees (your daughter demands a soda, which you refuse), finding a set of brick stairs. Your wife takes the stroller's handles while you hoist the other end, carrying your son down the stairs to the road like the Pope in his litter.

A donkey brays. You take photos of your family with the donkey's head peering over the fence. It stinks, so you move on.

Calves and thighs burning, you walk three abreast, blocking cars and tour buses as the descent steepens near the bridge. You pause several times going across to snap photos of the sweeping

views below and your wife as she tries to restrain your daughter from climbing over the railing to her death.

As the grade climbs, your pace slows. You wish you hadn't brought the heavy stuff, including one of your children. You pause several times to take photographs: of Civita, of the *agriturismi* and the neighboring towns around the valley rim. And, of course, your family.

Fellow tourists huff and puff about you, stopping for a cigarette to ease the journey as the smooth pavement turns into large cobbled stairs. In spite of an ever-steepening grade, you breathe a sigh of relief as you round the corner with the stroller (your wife gave up pushing it, so it's your duty now), drenched in sweat but seeing the end in sight.

Upon passing through the ancient gate (yes, you stopped to take photos before going through), you collapse for a moment in the shade, your children demanding water from the bottles you trucked along like pack mules. Around you sit equally sweaty and famished Italian, Australian, Chinese, French, and German tourists speaking over one another, a layering of native tongues.

As you enter Civita, you find a small *piazza* to your right (*Bellissima!* Snap, snap), a gift shop to your left (must remember to purchase *cartoline* on the way out), and the main *piazza*. Your daughter jumps into the dirt and drags large grooves with her feet across the *piazza* to the church, which is disappointingly under scaffolding.

You make note of Peppone's Bar on your right, a retail shop selling local olive oil and wine, and a *grotto bruschetteria*. As you move through Civita, you snap hundreds of photos: of ancient ovens, quaint stone buildings, and pink and red flowers in terracotta pots lining staircases up which you send your daughter for posed shots. Her squeals echo off the walls, as do your admonitions and your wife's complaints, punctuated by your son's shrieks when he spots each resident cat.

Peering in windows, you wonder where the people are. Civita is known as "the city that dies," so all these homes must be props...although the guide book promised there were seven to ten residents. You peer into gardens, not deterred by the blue *"Proprieta Privata"* sign, crunching around after your daughter in someone's gravel yard as you snap photos of the garden and three black cats until a gray-haired man emerges to shoo you away. You take photos of him and the young woman typing on a laptop at the table.

You pause for another cigarette, dropping the butt in the alley next to a deserted home, confused at the sound of opera music coming from above. So, someone lives here? While you are distracted your daughter pushes aside a wooden sawhorse to run into an open door. You command your wife to retrieve her. Again.

Finally, you dine *al fresco* at the small café bar next to Peppone's (their prices seemed high) after your daughter stomps her demand for lunch down the once-serene alley. The picturesque town has great views, but you wonder why anyone would live all the way up here where there are only cliffs, gardens, and weed tendrils curling around the walls.

Shame on you, I say! (And also, yikes.)

I arrived in Civita with a desire to look at how public and private life is carried out in Italy, and I realized that what exists elsewhere isn't necessarily true here. Turns out, when a place is billed as a dying city, people treat it as if there are no sacred spaces; everything is a quaint backdrop.

Much of what might otherwise be public life here is lived in private in order to block tourists from intruding on meals, times of tradition or repose, and family gatherings. Even when we attempt to stop them, *i touristi* walk into our homes and appear perplexed at our existence... and annoyance.

True, too, of last night's *Pizza nella Piazza* event, intended only for the Civitonici and certain "in the family" non-residents, like Father Marco. Still, there were tourists who tried to scam free wine and pizza. Tony gestured at their sly attempt as we watched them circle the *piazza* nonchalantly, saying to me, *"Loro fanno il Portoghese,"* referring to Italians who posed as Portuguese in the 18th Century to gain free admission to the Teatro Argentina in Rome.

I'll carry this lesson with me as I travel to Venice later this month, another apparent ghost town where life happens quietly above the street. In public, the tourist mob is smeared with *gelato* and sweat; in private, hundreds of stuccoed rooms with large ceilings and open windows exude sensuous aromas and sounds of people cooking, eating, laughing, loving, living, praying, and resting.

Of course, I hope someone there will let me crash.

Looking out on the ledge
of my neighbor's patio
after kitty scampered off.
Civita — 14. Aug

Nilde   gabi

Rainy Day Cat

Pitter pat comes the rain, belltower clang. The
week's first cool breeze sweeps in my door, spins
through *la cucina* and out my kitchen window.

Splattery splat, pitter pat, teeny tabby cat leaps
on my neighbor's stone wall to peer in.

Sonorous laughter, three friends *parlano italiano*
at the base of the stairs outside my door. *Allora,
magari, secondo me; loro mangiono insieme - uno, due,
tre.* Speaking of Civita's hush and the quickening
breeze, they squat at makeshift tables to eat picnic
fare while noisy *bambini* play streets away in
the square.

A distant bird's call arouses the cat, her searching
cry reaches my ears like a tortured violin, twisting
and contorting its strings. Breeze rustles her fur as
she mewls on the wall, blinking back at me as the
rain dabs her nose, **pitter splat**.

As I near, she starts, then stops cold—too curious
to flee.

Pitter splat, pitter splat, harder and faster the
rain. Wind begins to pick up and gusts in again.
Wood shutters clatter, the inner doors sucked
close with a slam. *Piano, piano,* tendril aromas of
oven fires tickle my nose and catch alight my
desire: *che il tempo per il pranzo*—time to eat lunch.

Splat, pat, pitter splat, away scampers the cat,
leaving me *da solo nella cucina,* no one to stare at.
Leaves fall heavy from the dampening rain while
rolling thunder echoes in booming refrain.

I stand a moment, awaiting her leaping return,
but I'm met only by raindrops on terracotta pots
and empty stone walls as my hunger stands facing
me there.

Two

"It's not a true inconvenience to act in accord with Mother Nature, but it shows how intimately tied to Nature we are."

27 Agosto: Cultivating Distance

Near and far, two chairs shaded by the canopy of an old oak tree. Swarming black flies, determined and cankered, infect our peace as Gaia, Maria and I arrive at *Hortus Unicorni*. Ito, lord and master of the gate, compliments our taste, bumping us with a gentle tickle from his broom-brush coat.

Luca, bearded and slight, blooms in our presence, turning open as his tour begins. He pours *espresso*, dark and rich like a secret—or his smoky laugh. Wet grass and weeds moisten my feet to the ankles, contrasted with the dry dust of Civita's *piazza* where scrapes are unforgiving and ankles twisted in an instant.

We are drawn across the manicured lawn by the hollow sound of water spilling from a bamboo pipe into the pond. Perhaps we're in Japan as we discover a shaded watery nook where plump orange-red koi flock and hunt lagoon fishes, waiting for Luca to caress their cold-blooded gills.

Hot and swampy like a Mississippi afternoon, sweat rivulets born at my temples glide down the angles of my cheeks to meet at my throat, pooling at the notch before disappearing all the way down to my toes. We cannot escape the flies and gnats, bees and mosquitoes—they shower us like waves of rice in a never-ending receiving line.

We find foreign bedfellows sharing an unlikely bower here: magnolias and citrus, Mediterranean *fiori* brilliant in color, strangling clematis and morning glory, swamp plants with fan leaves as large as a cape next to spiny African succulents, and a tree from India fruited with prayer beads.

Luca leads us through his pregnant Eden in white jeans and hair, tipped gray at the frame of his gently wrinkled but handsome face. He brings a cigarette to his smiling lips, but his jungle's fragrance is too potent for us to smell anything but loam, nectar, flowers, weeds, moss, and the perspiration of a million insects who pollinate his kingdom.

In a picture frame of leaves, I understand the concept of distance as Civita looms across the valley, bleached with haze. Her sun-baked stone bell tower has no voice here. A prelude to my temporary departure for Venice. Bearing thanks and praise, we lavish Luca with our best words before steering home, two mothers and their foreign daughter in the back seat.

Stepping towards Il Nuovo through the *piazza*, a familiar disgust rises at a tourist wearing only a black bra, a pyramid of tanned fat rolls one atop of each other, five high. *"Ciao, cara,"* says Nilde to me in passing, ignoring the spectacle.

Josè, out for a walk, is pleased at my description of Luca's giardino: *Bello, tranquillo,* and *molto meraviglioso. "Ciao, ciao; ci vediamo!"* she calls. I'm happy to be home.

What I thought was wild in Civita is tamed with the knowledge of Luca's jungle, coursing with animal will to escape its boundaries, concentric circles of order and chaos. Near and far, inside and outside, dust and mud, plump tomatoes and cloying vines.

A house in the valley and *un castello* on the hill. When my eyes search for Luca's garden from atop my aerie, the idea of it seems farther away still.

15 Agosto: A Sunday of New Rituals

My first Sunday in Civita is *Ferragosto*. For Catholics, today is the annual festival celebrating Mary's ascension into heaven, while in pagan times, it was a feast for Diana and a much-deserved rest from hard labor in the fields.

I found it amusing that, for pagans (and modern day Italians), it heralds a time of leisure and vacation, whereas the Roman Catholic Church named it, "a Holy Day of Obligation."

A tapestry of bells called me to mass with Tony, the second service I've attended in 18 years. In the secular bubble of Seattle, I often forget how seriously people elsewhere observe religion, but I was reminded of that when petite Josè arrived at Tony's gate to escort us to the Piazza del Duomo Vecchio wearing her fabulous green-tinted spectacles and very Italian Sunday best.

From our seat in the back pew, my eyes fell over this well-used church, once the site of an ancient Etruscan temple. The delicate frescoes on the ceiling have nearly vanished and the white-washed walls are in need of rehab (the exterior is currently under renovation), with tape marking where pictures once hung. Piled at the back are construction materials, draped tables with red prayer candles for sale, and a donation box next to the wooden double doors.

As I scanned the altar, outfitted in candles and cloth, I made out a glass coffin in which rests the body of S. Donato dressed in golden garb. Talk about obligation. Similarly, S. Bonaventure's arm resides in nearby Bagnoregio. Apparently, when you marry into the church, parts of you never leave for vacation, even at harvest time.

After mass, Josè (short for Guiseppina) invited me out for a coffee on Piazza Colesanti. In this small plaza, we watch people, mostly tourists, *fare una passagiata*. She asked what I thought of the service, to which I recalled the difference from attending mass with my mother as a child.

Listening to the priest deliver his sermon in Italian, hearing the 20 or so locals sing unfamiliar tunes, smelling the incense that we never used in my church—only when faced with these rituals in a foreign context did I conclude how truly foreign organized religion has always felt to me.

After we discussed my mother's family and the good weather (a complete reversal from yesterday's deluge and rough winds—*brutti venti*) Josè was interested to learn of my Italian heritage and the *cognomi* (surnames) of my grandparents. Soon after our *cappuccini al fresco*, I discovered why: she wished to tell my story to others.

During our walk home, I delighted in the sweet entwine of Josè's arm through mine. It felt very Italian that a 70-something woman who stands several inches shorter than me could lead me yet also use me for support in our trek through the tourists across the stones.

As we passed her fellow Civitonici, Josè paused to say in Italian, "May I present Gabriela Frank, an American writer who is a fellow with NIAUSI—she is one of Tony's. She is living in Civita for two months to write a book, and comes from an Italian family on her mother's side. She is learning Italian and would like to speak it with you when she's here."

After many smiles, handshakes and, utterances of, *"Piacere,"* I left Josè at her street and walked back alone to Il Nuovo, assuring her that I could find my way. I enjoyed feeling the tourists' inquisitive stares as I swept past them and up the stairs to begin in a new ritual: making lunch at home.

I sliced tomatoes and fresh buffalo mozzerella to make *caprese*, then cubed pecorino and parmesan cheese to accompany slices of *copacolla* and *pizza bianca*, baked dough brushed with olive oil and salt. Enjoying the sweet sunshine, I spent a leisurely hour consuming lunch while reading an Italian magazine, finally reaping the reward of many months of study.

After lunch, I wished myself *un buon Ferragosto*, which I've chosen to consider as a festival of sweet harvest: a reward of time, food, wine, experience, learning and growth—and with it, a bit of wonderment at which parts of me will always remain in Civita.

Three

"Details never escape Italian women; they know exactly what they're doing the moment they wake."

22 Agosto: The Feminine Mystique

It's Sunday in Civita, a day for traditions, including mass at 11:00 *ore*.

Before we enter, Tony rests momentarily on the long stone bench facing the *piazza*. There, Josè introduces me to Marcella, a 60-something woman with blond coiffed hair, gold-rimmed glasses, and a pearly smile. Marcella uses both hands to shake mine, and I do the same. I like her already. As more join the circle, I sit near Tony to observe the women in their finery.

Last night, Josè dazzled us with a yellow skirt, blue patterned blouse, two-toned ink-blue sweater that she knitted herself (she's always cold, even in the oppressive heat), and a beret—all this topped, naturally, by her tinted glasses. Though the side arcs of leather block the harsh light from her sensitive eyes, they succeed in appearing oh-so-stylish and, therefore, quintessentially Italian.

Today, Josè wears a delicate pigeon gray dress flocked with lavender-pink flowers, over which she has draped a pashmina of the same pink, a small kerchief-scarf around her neck and string of pearls with earrings to match. After the pearls catch my eye, I pick up the small white flecks in the pattern of her dress. Details never escape Italian women; they know exactly what they're doing the moment they wake.

During mass, as my eyes skip from the statue of Mary to *la bella figura* made by Josè, I begin to wonder about the gender of cities; are places like Civita inherently masculine or feminine?

After the service, I ask Josè if she would like to continue our tradition, *"Posso comprare a Lei un cappuccino alla piazza?"* We take our seats and our coffee, diving deep into conversation. Before walking home, we help Gaia send guests off with handshakes and advice on where to travel next. I enjoy the sensation of being warmly known, as Gaia lightly rests her hand on my back.

We opt to walk home along Civita's edge to enjoy the breeze and the view of the valley—a clearer path than dodging tourists on Via Mercatello. Sweetly, Josè links her arm through mine as we walk slowly, step by step, two women in possession of themselves and each another. Alternating English and Italian, we conclude our discussion of careers, men, Rome, Venice, and music.

Josè invites me to her home, which was renovated by Astra in the mid-1960s, her first project in Civita. She and Josè met through an architect, Malcolm Davis, though they realized that they had seen one another on a ship to Italy when Josè returned from Harvard.

The total ground area of Josè's home is tiny, perhaps 450 square feet, compactly nested among four stories. Dining room, kitchen and bathroom on the first floor, Josè's bedroom on the second, a sitting room on the third floor, and a fourth floor bedroom loft. The white-washed walls and wooden doors and window frames are familiar—it is, after all, an older sibling of Il Nuovo.

She noted a myriad of repurposed components, like the tall skinny window on the third floor that was once the means for residents to relieve themselves. (I shudder at the thought of sticking my backside outside a high window on an icy night, but they were tougher people back then.)

My favorite detail is the curved, deep sink built into the corner of the sitting room wall; once used for washing clothes, Astra retained it as an elegant architectural detail. She also punched interior windows to increase the flow of light and air, and gently molded nooks for shelves. Like I've appreciated of Il Nuovo, there is a palimpsest of fresh, feminine thoughtfulness atop age-old craft in this home.

On my afternoon walk, I happened upon Josè again, then outfitted in a blue scoopneck sundress, espadrille sandals, and a light straw hat banded with a dark ribbon. We greeted each other with cheek kisses, her skin soft and smooth against mine, as she said, *"Prendo il sole;"* I take the sun.

We discussed the homes next to hers, grand *palazzi* owned by wealthy men, both of whom are rarely in Civita to enjoy their rustic gardens or sweeping views. I considered how much of Civita's history—past and present—rests in Josè's mind; not only details and dates of architectural and cultural importance, but knowledge of her fellow Civitonici and their families, especially Astra and Tony.

As I returned to Il Nuovo, I heard a woman punctuate a sentence with, *"Mama mia!"* and her friend respond, *"Madonna,"* (always in two syllables: **MAH**-donna.) At that moment, Civita's utter femininity revealed itself to me...

...In her *grotti* and hidden places, a series of wombs.

...In her fertile *giardini*, whose crops nourish and shade us, like a mother.

...In her *chiesa* where the statue of Mary is revered center stage, and in whose name the main gate is christened.

...In her green edges, clinging vines, and *fiori* that soften even the hard, ancient stone.

...In her tempests, an exasperated *donna* who cries furious tears, then is tender and soothing again.

...In Astra, who was pivotal in respecting and rebuilding a place abandoned by men.

...In Josè, who bridges the worlds of yesterday and today.

And, I realize, in women like me, who pick up where Astra and Josè leave off. Perhaps, we Fellows and our work can be considered the progeny, a renewing legacy, of these potent feminine forces: Mary, Astra, Josè, Maria, Domenica, Gaia, Vittoria, Nature—and Civita.

26 Agosp: A Sacred Circle

The concept of a circle is both wholeness and a new beginning. The ancients considered circles to represent the idea and power of God, which we might describe as both infinite and divine.

Circles draw safe boundaries; they create places where one can enter and join something bigger than herself. Some call this faith or religion, but last night under the light of *una bella luna,* we called it dance.

Coinciding with Astra's birthday was a town fest featuring a locally-grown musician, Salvatore Archangeli, who specializes in music...and interior remodeling. He and his family joined our large group for dinner at Osteria al Forno di Agnese where Josè and Marcella worked their collective magic as mistresses of ceremonies. Joining us were Gaia and Bernardo, Maria (a singer whom everyone calls Maria di Venezia), Father Marco, Tony, Iole Alessandrini, and my across-the-way neighbor, Nilde.

Very quickly, I felt alien amongst this group due to my limited (though growing) Italian language skills. In contrast to the one conversation at Gaia and Bernardo's dinner table, last night was a social din—many conversations in quick Italian, all at once, demanding immediate attention. I felt self-conscious when someone spoke to me, as they were often forced to slow down, repeat themselves, and gesture as though I was a child.

In all of this, I appreciated the no-nonsense way Nilde, sitting at my left, took ownership of me, addressing me as, "Americana," in a gruffly affectionate way. As I indicated my wine preference, she reached over the other Italians, calling out, *"La signorina americana preferisce rosso!"* to make sure that I had a decent splash before it was taken in the frenzy. She did the same as the food was passed around: lightly battered and fried zucchini flowers, fried cheese with anchovy, shredded beef with arugula and pine nuts, and grilled eggplant. *More?* she'd ask. *"Perché no?!"* I replied.

Apart from simple dialogue describing my family background and why I'm in Civita, I said little during dinner and was eager to escape to the *piazza* as the music began. As I exited the frenetic patio of the *osteria*, the first full moon of my stay loomed large in the sky. Believing I was amongst strangers, I moved to sit off to the side, but felt a flash of delight as Bernardo flagged me over.

The next thing I knew, they were all there around me: gorgeous Maria in her yellow ombre dress; elegant Gaia in a floor-length summer gown; and Marcella unleashing that sweet, lusty laugh that said she was ready for a good time. Alessio, a young shoe designer from Florence, came by with plastic cups and jug wine, a necessary ingredient for any bacchanal.

I couldn't keep from grinning when several women were inspired to groove to a tune I can only describe as the Italian Chicken Dance. Song after song, Salvatore played for the Civitonici, joined by flocks of tourists and visitors from Bagnoregio, who spun across the *piazza*, often in same-sex couples since women seem to outnumber men in both life expectancy and mobility.

Alessio promenaded with Alessandra, evoking transfixed stares from her sons, Ludivico and Giovanni, while Marcella and Iole waltzed together with laughter, unsure who was leading. As I watched from my perch between Bernardo and Nilde on the stone bench in front of Peppone's Bar, a feeling of quiet melancholy whispered underneath the accordion music: *I don't fit in here.*

Without warning, Marcella took my hand and Maria's at the beginning of the next song, turning us into a circle that grew quickly with Alessandra and Alessio, Iole and Gaia, and others who couldn't resist joining our circle dance.

Like pagans, we reeled one way and then the other, our skirts flying about us like ceremonial robes. Alessio broke the circle to dance under the joined hands of Gaia and Alessandra, and we all followed suit into a snakelike conga line, turning wildly this way and that until we joined hands to form the circle again.

The more we laughed, the faster our circle turned, and the more vigorously Salvatore played. We danced and danced until finally—panting, laughing, and spent—we collapsed to drink more wine, an ancient ceremony for modern times.

After a nearly embarrassing moment with Father Marco (priests get handshakes, not kisses!), I bid everyone goodnight, finding countless warm embraces from new friends.

I realized that, in experiencing what the ancient Greeks called *ekstasis* and *enthusiasmos* during our dance, I began to better understand the true meaning—and sacred power—of a circle.

Inside that circle, I felt invited, like I belonged.
Inside that circle, we did not need words to communicate.
Inside that circle, we held hands without reservation.
Inside that circle, we found freedom of expression and the ability to make and break forms.
Inside that circle, ten strangers became a single, unified idea that had no beginning or end.

Some people might call that divine.

A City Grows Here

Sand-colored tufa, celadon leaves of wisteria, grapevines and fruiting trees. Woven together down staircases and through arbors and porches, the two are inseparable in Civita, a paradise in the clouds.

Who's to say whether the stones rise out of the gardens, or if the gardens grow from the stones? Inseparable, entwined, they brace one another: the vine holds the bricks at the edge, and the bricks invite the vines to grow, to splay across them.

Who can number the lives that take place inside those green palaces? Bumblebees so big they shouldn't be able to fly, though nature forgot to tell them so (or perhaps they refused to listen.) Wasps, mosquitoes, moths, and flies buzz in and out of the vines while beetles and spiders nestle in hidden earthy nooks.

Who knows how many residents a stone home can hold? Scorpions live there, emerging for midnight strolls. Smarter than some, they cling to the wall, inviting neither love nor tragedy. We've made peace for now, my scorpion and I; *si chiama* Ortenzio, and we've agreed on separate quarters. In good faith, I've offered him the opportunity to observe me at his pleasure, so long as he doesn't become fresh.

Who's to guess at how many meals these gardens provide? Insects work both soil and flowers that burst forth our *pomodori* and lettuce, cucumbers and *basilico*, and—most importantly— *il nostro vino*. Each outcropping of stones holds a garden that holds meals which hold families; together the gardens and stone hold our lives.

Tony's five turtles nod in agreement from their sunny rocks.

Who can guess how something simple like shade feeds our relationships? Arbors make patios for dining *al fresco* while benches make seats for rest. Secret stone inlets tapestried in vines are places for lovers to share stolen moments. While the shade lasts, they are not mother or father, neither son nor granddaughter, but people in love, fighting the knowledge that someone will cry for their attention soon, breaking the spell.

Who can determine which holds more fidelity, the intractable tufa or the supple greenery? They've grown together for so long that each bears qualities of the other: the tufa holds water and permits tendrils to grow within its cracks, while vines and stumps petrify with age, clinging to the very walls they support, reinforcing that ancient strength with new life ever-growing.

Remove the stones, and there's no place for gardens; remove gardens and there's no life in the stones. Young and old, flowering green plants and cool gray bricks, in sun and in shadow they play for us a series of perfect and never-ending foils.

Insects crawl in and fly out of these places, momentary pestilent reminders that, without nature in the city, no city can remain.

Four

"Civita doesn't feel like an eerily preserved amusement park of ancient spirits, but a very approachable, livable, time-honored place that actually has a future."

16 Agosto: It's Your Turn

"Oh, Gabriela, this is the experience that you'll write about!" cries Alessandra, partly serious. A friend of Tony's and a fellow architect, she's describing the chaos that surrounds her as the single mother of two energetic young boys, Giovanni and Ludivico.

When they arrived at Tony's for dinner last night, I recognized them from church, recalling their inability to sit still. Under her dark brown hair, Alessandra's olive skin is perfect—save for the circles under her eyes, which speak to her lack of sleep—or time to eat or bathe in peace.

Dark like his mother, Giovanni is a year older than 4-year-old Ludivico, though both are slight of build. I marveled at the way they burst through Tony's gate, dragging their feet to kick deep grooves in his gravel. After pursuing his cats around the yard, Ludvi required Tony's rescue after he climbed on top of the roof and enthusiastically attempted to jump off while we were inside preparing dinner.

Alessandra invited us to lunch at her parents' house today, just around the corner from Tony's. We climbed the stairs and into their lovely home with exposed stone walls and a small eat-in kitchen. Amazingly, nothing was broken—including bones—as the boys tumbled in and out onto the stone stairs, taking turns refusing to eat the wonderful food that Alessandra prepared, including a zucchini and basil *risotto* tinted with tomato, followed by *pollo con salvia* pounded thin.

Inside her family life, I recognized the same hardships that exist for my single-parent friends in the States: providing 24/7 supervision, encouraging/tricking the kids to eat, disciplining them, and struggling to remain a nurturer, caregiver, and breadwinner.

They call Civita the dying city, but I don't agree. Watching the many children who stay here—Fabrizio's daughter, Gaia's grandchildren, Alessandra's boys, Antonio's grandchildren—I realized that there is an ongoing heartbeat embodied in a new generation of young people. Like the rest of private life in Civita, the heirs-apparent are simply kept from display during their childhoods.

Sitting in her parents' kitchen, it felt intimate to see Alessandra revealed in a naked light, to hear her exhausted appeal, watching her light a cigarette on the stove's flame and lean back with a deep sigh to finish her *espresso*. "Oh, Tony, Gabriela, do you see how it is?" she asks. "What else can I do?"

Blond Ludivico continued to add wine to his water and rise from his seat after repeated admonitions from his mother. A swift smack didn't dissuade either boy from struggling loudly over a toy. From the serene streets, one couldn't guess that all of this life was happening inside a "dead" city.

I thought back to the card game I played with the boys last night, during which they only said two words to me, *"Tocca te,"* (your turn) with quiet reservation, since I was still a stranger at that point. As Alessandra came by to see how our game was going, I asked, *"Come si dice 'shy' in italiano?"*

She eyed her two boys, knowing that there were only temporarily demure. She shook her head, answering, "In Italian, there's no such word."

When these boys are grown up enough to take their turn, to bring their own families back to Civita, I'll bet they won't be shy about it one bit.

18 Agosto: Civita Sings The Blues

The original goal for my work in Civita was to consider its sustainability from a different point of view. Not obvious metrics, such as average carbon footprint per resident—or, better said, not in the way that others might consider these measures. My intent was to promote an understanding of sustainability through the lens of lifestyle: a personal, experiential first-hand account that would speak to people in an emotional rather than technical way.

My interest rests in uncovering the sustainability of this lifestyle in terms of relationships, connectivity, culture, economics, resilience, health and happiness. Measuring energy load or water consumption may reveal a building's performance, and life cycle cost analysis can speak to economics, however if we ignore human emotional complexity—such things as contentment, which can appear difficult or too "soft" to bother measuring—we're missing the boat.

Last night, I began to address one rather broad question: What makes great urban places timeless?

When sitting in the *piazza* listening to live jazz echoing around the stone buildings, the answer—people—seemed obvious. The life and vitality of Civita or any great urban place always comes back to humans and their necessities that layer new on top of old.

A striking natural and constructed venue, Civita provides a compelling stage for such a marriage of old and new. A rich context of palimpsest is what calls people here thousands of years later. Still, I felt surprised and touched to hear modern American music performed in a truly ancient place, enjoyed by Italians young and old.

With such thoughts, I considered how ancient music itself is; humans have always found ways to make joyful noise. It was true of the Etruscans who first settled in Civita (they played pan-flutes, strings, and drums) and it was true of last night's ensemble, who played the blues with electric guitars on the dirt floor of the *piazza* in front of the church.

Watching the crowd, mostly from Bagnoregio (which means they made a long, dark, steep trek home afterward), I thought of the human need to gather, not just families or friends, but strangers. Being a social species is what has helped us to survive for thousands of years; separation is not only a punishment, it can depress us and destroy our human nature.

While being apart can tear us down, one thing that never fails to cheer us is dance. Moving in between the warm yellow and cool blue stage lights, the Italians swayed and danced together as if jazz was their own. Two tots sitting on the stone step next to me jumped up when encouraged by the lead singer, reminding me that there's no escaping our genetic urge for expression through physical movement, especially with each other.

The viability of human places is based on the dance of our relationships and our shared rituals; without ties, we move on. As humans, we have a deep-seated need to matter and be able to affect the world—we desire to be seen and known.

I greeted Gaia and Ilaria after the concert, finding warm hugs and kisses from both. After I dropped them off at their door, I walked through the pools of amber lamplight, exploring the quiet that suddenly fell. There were only the sounds of my shoes on the stones and the cool, sweet-smelling air on my skin...and Nerone who meowed at me, welcoming me home. Other innate needs—fresh air, privacy and feline companionship—are equally as ancient as Civita itself.

To me, sustainability boils down to time: how long can anything—food, money, oil, clean air, cities, love—sustain us? The reinvigoration of any resource, whether it's a foodshed or a relationship, is part of its sustainability. That, partnered with how well we acknowledge our enjoyment or appreciation of it—the feeling that makes us continue doing or protecting something—is what defines how long that resource exists.

With time is also necessary the ability to grow, change, adapt, rebuild, and love—or die. Say, isn't that what jazz is all about?

25 Agosto: A Sense of Soul

For a place known as "the city that dies," one that visitors indeed treat as a ghost town, Civita does not feel a bit haunted—in spite of the bodies resting inside glass coffins on the church's altar.

I've spent the past week considering the concept of after-image or "collective soul" in ancient places, positive that, after more than 2,000 years, there must be a specter lurking in someone's *cantina*. Yet, all I've found in Civita is quiet repose and animated conversation. (In Italy, is there any other kind?)

This morning, as Tony, Gaia, Iole, and I set out to visit Astra's grave in honor of her birthday, I sifted through a few stories about her life and her work in Civita. Indeed, her architectural interventions quite deftly build upon and carefully reveal the past, employing a consistent and honest

ASTRA ZARINA
1929 2008

palette that recognizes traditional materials and function. This, wedded with clean, modern materials, gives her designs a fresh sense of re-purpose, including Josè's home, which Astra renovated over 40 years ago.

This carefully revealed layering is, in fact, the very reason that Civita does not feel like an eerily preserved amusement park of ancient spirits, but a very approachable, livable, time-honored place that has a future.

When I learned that Astra and Tony first lived in Lo Studio for years before they constructed the home where Tony now resides, I realized how very unaware I am as to the degree in which these homes—and Civita as a whole—were destroyed and crumbling. Il Nuovo, the newest NIAUSI acquisition and the home in which I live, fits so well with Lo Studio and Il Ruderino, that I cannot imagine these homes weren't always linked.

Then, there is Tony's home where he and Astra lived together for years. When I asked him to describe a project from his career of which he felt most proud, he said it was the design of their pergola—the perfect place for dining under grapevines. The pergola's arches, I discovered, are actually the last remaining portion of the exterior of a home that once stood on the property. They look like they were spirited from a Roman ruin, although I had assumed that they were fabricated specifically for the pergola because they fit the space so ideally. Evidence again of how authentically revealed—and well used—the past is here.

Iole described how she met Astra by serendipity when they separately pursued a design competition in Rome during the early 90s. She couldn't ignore the coincidence that they had each arrived at an eerily similar solution, though they didn't know one another. Feeling a sense of connection through their parallel approaches, Iole sought out Astra and was instantly drawn to both her and Tony. From my perspective, she is in many ways like a daughter to them, carrying their lessons into her work today, including her involvement with NIAUSI.

We spoke little as we visited Astra's resting place, high above the ground. Tony brought a single fuchsia rose from their garden, which he kissed before handing it to Iole to place next to Astra's name. It didn't escape me that the lettering for her marker was rendered in a simple face under which bears only the years of her life. No flowery quote, no specific dates.

Even Astra's grave—with its single rose—stands as an example of exquisite, elegant design.

Story after story, I feel like I'm coming closer to understanding the profound effect that Astra has made in Civita. She was an integral force in the continued transformation and revealing of this cultural asset as a place for study, connection, introspection, and repose.

Finishing this essay in the common space between Il Nuovo and Lo Studio, I jumped when the door behind me opened slowly and inexplicably—the wind, perhaps. Yet, hairs on the back of my neck stood up when the front door followed suit seconds later, opening on its own a space just large enough for a person to exit through.

Perhaps I was wrong, and there are indeed spirits residing in Civita. *Buon compleanno,* Astra.

26 Settembre: Finding Religion

From age six, I knew that organized religion was not for me.

Raised in the Catholic faith by my mother, I dabbled in Judaism through my father's side of the family, mostly through meals growing up, and later through a college course. Both traditions seemed like good metaphors, but never something that I could—or needed to—believe in as a saving grace, reason for existence, or justification for good or evil.

I remember staring up at Father Jack (my favorite priest, he was always kind to us kids, especially during confession) as he read his sermon, thinking, "I can't believe that these adults pretend to believe in this."

Not long after, I realized that they weren't the ones pretending; I was. I carried on this illusion until I turned 18.

My mother wanted to see me confirmed in the church. After she died in my teens, I made sure to honor her wish, even though it meant nothing to me. In fact, it was burdensome to engage in a religion that I didn't agree with, but I did so because I believed in my mother. The name I took as my confirmation name, long forgotten until this moment as I write it, was her middle name, Kay, because it was more about her faith than my own.

These thoughts surfaced today when my sister-out-law, Kirstin, asked me during mass if I planned to take communion. I quipped, "If I did, I'd probably burst into flame."

Since I was 18, the only other time I've been to mass prior to Civita was in 2007 when I attended a service in Montreal's Notre Dame cathedral. This is especially poignant, since I've witnessed two baptisms in the past two days: Antonio and Rossana's *nipota*, Elena, was baptized yesterday afternoon, and Laura and Roberto's *figlio*, Alberto, was baptized during this morning's mass.

The invitation to Elena's baptism was indeed an honor, and a special treat. The *chiesa* was brilliantly lit, and the configuration of pews changed in order to center the ceremony around the revealed fresco of Mary—a panel that lay hidden until an earthquake in the 1600s. The parishioners prayed to be saved from the natural disaster, and underneath the very walls of their seemingly well-known church, a new vision of Mary spontaneously appeared from beneath the plaster just as the ramifications of the quake subsided. Naturally, this was declared a miracle.

As we entered the church, still humbly cloaked under scaffolding, my heart warmed to see Elena's name written in flowers that splayed in a sunburst on the floor near Miracle Mary. My camera failed during the ceremony, so I was only able to capture her name on the floor, but I wondered if that somehow wasn't a sign, too; perhaps some things are meant to be described in stories and metaphors rather than with physical proof.

I considered that during this morning's mass, as Laura, who comes from the valley surrounding Civita, brought her family, friends, and her childhood priest, who now serves a parish in Genoa, back to Civita for her son's baptism.

Laura helps Tony with the upkeep of his house and all of the NIAUSI properties; only today did I learn of her familial ties with Civita. For her, this place is a Mecca to which it is important for family to return at special moments. Though she may not be considered "Civitonici" as much as Antonio and Rossana, who live and work here, I see a powerful affinity between her son, Alberto, and Elena: baptism in Civita. They and their families will always return here. That I was lucky enough to be present for both events, I cannot fathom.

For hours afterwards, I thought of how many people are born in this place, and the different creeds they are born into. Some are born into Catholicism or descendant families, others into architecture and urban design, and still others into the religion of *la vita bella italiana*.

Tonight, as we enthusiastically stuffed zucchini flowers with mozzarella and anchovies for dinner, I felt so grateful that, on their maiden exploration, my out-laws Sue and Kirstin have been quickly initiated into the lives, food, customs, and traditions of this very unique Italian hill town.

While I may not practice an organized religion, I most certainly believe in the power of devoted people, and there is no shortage of them here. Seeing families and friends trek up the bridge to gather around Elena and Alberto allowed me to witness Civita in yet another way: as an iconic place of faith even in the modern day.

Watching Father Marco laugh with surprise abandon during Elena's baptism as she fussed, I thought: there's more hope married within the bones of this place than is apparent, even after living here for a month and a half. Though I feel like a small part of Civita, I'm still an outsider; it would take a lifetime to truly understand how these families have grown—and will continue to do so—over generations.

I may not be able to probe anyone's wounds, but seeing these baptisms has restored my faith a bit. I suppose it goes back to my belief in the power of people, and knowing that there are many of us gathered here and abroad who care about preserving Civita.

In fact, if I had to choose, I'd say that people are ultimately my religion. To some, that could be considered a miracle.

Civita Escapes in the Wind

La tempesta prima festa, vines buck and hitch like a mare refusing to be broken. Sun glares without warming, no clouds before it, a false smile with no heat of friendship shining behind. Shutters clatter, clang, and batter stucco into smithereens, another part of Civita too easily swept away. Thwarted by wind, damned flies gather again inside kitchens of housewives who shoo them away.

Burdened washer women sneeze as they transport their linens, walking through pollen clouds, thick yellow dragons that breathe spores of fire, inflaming their lungs. Piqued pussy cats chase leaves that scatter and run like phantom mice; their capricious prey skips left and right before each fruitless pounce. They lay low to the ground, ears pricked and tails down, as the gusts blow their fur aside to reveal tender pink skin.

Alleys become wind tunnels, conducting a rushing reverberation, channeling the tempest around our *piazza* like thundering cheers circling an arena. Whirring drafts penetrate windows and gates as the high-pitched wind whines. Long-legged spiders, limbs thin as thread, blow over rooftops, tangled in their own ruined architecture—next to the meals they were about to eat.

Returning birds, blown off course and confused, are grounded as they search for their aeries, incapable of overcoming the windshear to take flight. Shards of terracotta, blown over and broken, spew spilled soil like fractured promises, all in a row on the wall.

Fifty-foot pines bend to the might of the wind, threatening in waves to fall like their pinecones that litter the stones. Birds and insects, cats and man and plants, all at unease with these unstoppable waves.

The tower bell chimes three times, as if to announce the next round of a prize fight, while we're left to decide whether to quit or press on. Flags tattered and wrapped, we're hopelessly trapped— outmatched by Civita herself as her dust rains blows unchecked by our insulted skin. Refusing to concede, we're drawn to the *piazza* where there are festival races at hand, wrapped in our rags like a train of nomads.

Ruthless dust devils sweep bits of tufa away, assaulting us with ancient grit, coating every surface with grains of history. Whipping wind scrapes the buildings—enraged—but perhaps someday Civita will gather and grow at a river's confluence, accumulating over a thousand years to make another Civita some place far away.

via Porta
S. maria
—— Civita
2010

Gabri

Five

"If it were more accessible, would it still be civita?"

13 Agosto: Building Bridges

If life were a bridge, it would be bound by clear endings and beginnings, broadcast its reach and grade, and reveal obstacles in plain sight. One could gauge the energy of a lifespan before taking a breath.

In Civita, walking up and down *il ponto* each day is a choice to be—or not be—connected with the rest of the world. With planning, it's possible to subsist for days without returning to Bagnoregio, something necessary when a storm arrives. While not impossible to cross the causeway during a thunder storm, it is ill-advised and has, on occasion, been fatal.

Today, Tony and I made our shopping for the weekend in advance of the storm, now rolling in late on a Friday afternoon. Knowing that Saturday, when the full force of the storm will hit, would be the only weekend day when food is available for purchase, we opted to shop early this morning and stay tucked inside *domani*.

The only other time I've done such a thing was during Seattle's epic snow storms of 2008, which demonstrates how different daily routines are in Civita. It's not an inconvenience to act in accord with Mother Nature, but it shows how intimately tied to Nature we are. It also reveals how convenient my life—and many people's lives—are back home; we exist under a fragile illusion of food security.

Real and metaphoric bridges open and close in perpetual motion, depending on the weather, on one's physical ability to climb the causeway or carry a load of groceries, or on the availability of services here or in town from day to day.

Taking time to consider these things from the perspective of the Civita experience—to reflect and act on relationships with humans, the built environment, and Nature—requires a higher level of patience and a slower speed than many modern lives typically afford.

To escape from the rain, I sat within the Porta S. Maria, Civita's main gate at the top of the bridge, to sketch and observe travelers. It occurred to me that the bridge, which divides Civita from Bagnoregio, from Lazio, from the world, is the same device that also connects it with people from every continent. Today alone, travelers from Italy, Germany, the United States, Brazil, Australia, and Canada passed by me as my pen flew across the page in rapid strokes.

A dichotomy is true of all bridges: they create distance, but they also connect. In this way, Civita's bridge has created an unprecedented retreat for me. Yet, in taking a pause from the U.S., from speaking English, and from my day job, I've been able to connect with people and life here in ways that I'm glad I couldn't foresee: from growing dialogue with Corrine, a June-born Cancerian, who makes delicious *cappuccini* at Peppone's Bar, or Fabrizio, a winemaker and owner of an *agriturismo* in the valley below Civita.

Without knowing, I've been drinking Fabrizio's wine each night at dinner with Tony, and had occasion to discuss it with him today when he dropped by the *sala grande*. Since Fabrizio speaks very little English, I was again encouraged by circumstance to reach deeply into what I've learned from *la mia insegnanta*, and expand out with my language "bridge" to connect with someone.

Like the Civitonici, in crossing the span each day, I choose to be apart from life outside. Yet, I'm also encouraging an inner life to grow: an emerging voice that considers Civita's form, function, and identity in order to create a bridge of another kind—one that connects new hearts and minds to this special place through the powerful link of storytelling.

24 Agosto: Inside /Outside

I've quickly learned that what I consider to be hot weather is merely warm to the Civitonici, although the word Italians use for warm actually translates as "hot," as in, *Fa caldo*. That said, we all agree that the weather of late has been *caldissimo*. For days, our shutters have remained closed, our interior spaces dark, and our food at room temperature. We move less, we sweat more, and I've learned not to drag groceries uphill on foot from Bagnoregio when it's over 90° F.

Watching all of us dissolve to our interiors was as curious as watching this morning's refreshing, ghostly fog envelop Civita, turning the city inside in a completely different way. With time and heat, the fog burned off by noon, but the day turned out more temperate than it has been.

Pairs of opposites innate to Civita—continuity/change, hot/cool, tourist/resident, fog/sun—ask me to consider how internal and external forces work here. By turning inside, are we making an intentional choice to turn away from the outside world? How much of that density within a community leads to a purer sense of identity, and how much is xenophobic navel gazing? If one decides to step outside, how does Civita look from there?

To answer these questions, I strolled out of the main gate and down the bridge, observing my gait as I descended down the steep grade. For two weeks, I've pounded up and down this climb, partly to escape the heat and use my time well, and partly to avoid blending in with the tourists.

This trip, my feet enjoyed sensing the curves between the stones as I made my way down, sure-footed as a donkey. I didn't blow past people, nor was my pace intentionally slow; it simply felt *proprio*. The breeze picked up, dropping the intensity of the late afternoon blaze, and I felt in balance and in charge of my destiny.

From the end of the *ponte* looking back at Civita, seemingly perched precariously on top of the hill, I listened as people began and ended their tours. On approach, they consistently displayed a sense of bracing and awe; on return, most seemed quiet and reflective, as if they absorbed some of Civita's internal focus.

At that, I realized how things are beginning to change in my mind. I don't feel like a tourist or visitor any longer, though I'm far from being a resident. Day and night, I'm finding a rhythm that works somewhere in the middle. In fact, I believe that the extreme dichotomies unique to this place—challenging topography and access, closeness to nature (animal, vegetable...insect), pedestrian transportation, the weather, historic buildings, lush and edible gardens, new ways of preparing food, and certainly, the people—are what is bringing me closer to a fluid center.

After two weeks in Civita, my initial awe is beginning to lift, revealing an opportunity see more clearly, and investigate these principles more deeply. I'm learning how this immersive experience allows one to first contract inside, then expansively explore these opposites, and ultimately find the common meaning within them.

In my fellowship proposal, I wondered how Civita is relevant to our modern lives. One way to answer that would be to ask in return, how can we live *without* rare places such as Civita, where time and exposure not only alter living rock, but also soften, expand, and reveal a deepening inner humanity within people like me who come here to observe, learn and grow?

29 Agosto: Finishing The First Course

Few things are as strange as leaving for mass on a peaceful Sunday morning knowing that there will be *paparazzi* at the base of my stairs. At this point in my Civita experience, I know to have my sunglasses in place upon opening my door to make the proper entrance onto the red carpet.

Outside the tourist spotlight, I bask in the pleasure I receive from my Sunday rituals: waiting in the shade on the step just inside Tony's gate, and our *piano, piano* pace as we step to church, often joined by Josè, who takes my arm. I delight in meeting the ladies and walking inside together. I relish hearing Father Marco's soft timbre as he sings during mass. I especially enjoy gathering afterward for *aperitivi alla piazza* so that I can hear and practice Italian.

Father Marco honored Astra during today's service, the second anniversary of her death. He noted her accomplishments in the restoration and study of Civita, as well as her cultural and social contributions to the community. Afterwards, a large crowd gathered to toast her spirit: Tony, Gaia and Bernardo, Ilaria, Josè, Marcella, Maria, Laura and her husband, Roberto, Marco and his wife, Inga, and Peppi, who arrived all in black. His outfit earned the teasing title of *Padre Peppi*.

With a round-robin of *chin-chins* and *salutes*, some of us quaffed *prosecco* while others took their bitters with soda water and ice. Discussion turned quickly to local politics over adding vehicle transport in and out of Civita. (A growing number of older residents are incapable of making the trip up and down the bridge without assistance.)

Considering how much time I've spent in seclusion at the top of the hill due to the heat, I agree that access—even for we, the young and able-bodied—can be a bother. Trekking from here to Bagnoregio and back carrying 25 pounds of groceries on foot under the August sun is prohibitive. This challenge speaks to the livability of Civita; yet, if it were more accessible, would it still be Civita? I wondered how it would factor into my life if I chose to live here.

As debate continued, I beat Josè to the punch by paying for everyone's drinks. How else could I thank them for the kindnesses that they've shown to me? Josè was so overcome that she insisted on taking me to lunch, saying that I should save my money for Venice. That's how I found myself *pranzando al fresco* on the shaded patio of Osteria d'Agnese with Josè, Maria, and Marcella, who finally said the phrase that I've been dying to hear since I arrived: *"Dammi del tu!"*

Marking a key turning point in a relationship, this phrase demonstrates a level of comfort and affection, declaring a preference to be addressed informally as, *"tu"* rather than using the formal, *"Lei."* In fact, it is customary to continue using the formal address—no matter how many times you have interacted with someone—until he or she explicitly commands you to, "Give me the *'tu!'"*

Upon hearing Marcella's words, and feeling Maria gently caress my cheek, I decided that there is no more fitting way to leave Civita for a few days. Reflecting on the past three weeks, I've felt this place and her people guide me to a more introspective way that I consider to be "Part One" of this journey.

I may have set the table for this adventure, but these experiences have made this *primo* course both flavorful and nourishing to the body, heart, mind, and spirit.

As I wrote notes for today's essay, I decided to leave my front door open, music playing in the background, and sit in plain view on my stoop. It was a different interaction from writing behind Tony's gate or in the cool darkness of my kitchen. I considered it an invitation to both the tourists and myself; an explicit declaration: "I live in this house and I am a part of this community."

While I'm in Venice attending the Biennale, I will be thinking about what I want the second course to be. My instinct says that it will be even more interactive, now that I've moved through the initial cultural boundaries and—for the duration of this fellowship, at least—made a true mental separation from life before Civita.

Who's to say what I'll discover upon my return—what questions I'll ask, what characteristics will reveal themselves, how I'll continue to change with the experience, or what surprises await.

Perhaps the only thing that's sure is that my second helping of Civita will be even more flavorful than the first.

Intermezzo

"Iole and I softly agreed at how difficult it would be to return to the world—after all, when one knows that places like Venezia or Civita exist, how can There be anything else?"

A Pause

Not knowing ahead of time the impact it would have, I took a brief pause from Civita to meet Iole in Venice for the architecture Biennale. This intermission afforded me a new perspective, allowing me to compare the two cities and mark a transition between my first month in Civita and the second.

When I re-entered the Porta S. Maria only five days later, I could see the person I was when I first walked through that gate on August 10—and an idea of the woman I hoped to become when I exited through it in October. The combined effect of time, adventure, language, food, new friendships, and the experience of two beloved cities had set a transformation in motion.

Coincidentally, by the time I returned, most of the vacationing Civitonici had left for their permanent homes in Rome, Florence, and beyond. Though I would see several of my favorites again in Rome just before I left for home, I felt their absence for the duration of my stay in Civita… and to the present.

In Dreams, Venezia

Venezia is a dream—a voyage that begins where the train tracks end—the wide, white smile of a friend who embraces you with soft arms, cool breezes, and cerulean skies. Four gondoliers doff their ribboned hats to enjoy a snack at the table next to yours, crustless white *tramezzini* filled with *prosciutto* and *carciofi* that disappear in seconds—then so do they.

Vaporetti ferry you from bank to bank with grinding motors that shift abruptly in reverse, water churning about, and bump against the floating docks with a quake and a see-saw bob that remains with you for minutes on land. You follow old white signs in dialect leading from *campo* to *rio* to *via* to *ponte* to *calle* to *fondamente*; some are streets now where water once ran. Churches abut hotels next to homes with ground-floor restaurants followed by shoe shops, book shops, and clothing shops; *negozio* after *negozio*.

In the market after noon, the odor of today's catch lingers in fishy ice that's hosed to the floor drains. Columns with ichthyian capitals stand guard over a sea of vendors' umbrellas where one can buy soft green figs, plump red tomatoes, and brilliant saffron-colored *fiori di zucca* for breading and frying.

Bent old women weave through the crowd, arms laden with plastic sacks like bracelets from wrist to elbow. *Carabinieri*, always in pairs, glide along in smartly tailored olive-green uniforms to monitor a peace that appears ever-kept.

When thousands of strolling couples make the late afternoon *passagiata*, you have a front seat complete with salty potato chips and balloon goblets of *spritz*. The tangy liquid-sun flavor of *aperol* tempered by cool white wine and sparkling water meets your lips as you suck gently on the shipwrecked slice of orange, pregnant with juice.

Waves of ultramarine, violet, and burnt orange layer the sky as the setting sun falls behind the buildings. Canal-side, there are white tablecloths and pitchers of young, sweet wine—and a fleet of mosquito captains in pursuit of your blood. Fried *cichetti*—red peppers, shrimp, calamari, zucchini—flavored with salt and oil gently tease out the wine's flavor.

Sulphuric lamp light effects a soft glow as the crowds wane. A roving guitarist with charcoal skin picks gently while his partner's serenade of, *"O Sole Mio,"* elicits coins from a couple who desire neither their music nor their company.

Tobacco and marijuana smoke tickle your nose. Smoky tendrils weave above your head like genies in the darkness as you disappear down an alley barely as wide as your frame.

A short, bullish man with salt and pepper hair brushes past you as he exits his antiquities shop, close enough to see the curly tufts of black hair that spring from his ears. *"Dimmi,"* he gently growls into his phone, turning the ancient key and walking home. The lagoon water relaxes from blue-green to inky black. When you look up, the fingernail moon greets you in the company of all the stars you can't see at home.

Your feet tire stone by stone, stair by stair, bridge by bridge, but Venezia only becomes more interesting as the darkness thickens. You happen on archways filled with graffiti and couples embracing in the corner; a tiny *campo* with bars still open past *l'uno* gather crowds like moths to a flame. Distracted by a throng of college students singing "Blowin' in the Wind," you nearly miss the friar frocked in warm brown robes. He darts from one *calle* to the next, lithe like a cat, then disappears.

Venezia is a dream sweetly held in old rugs and crumbling stucco, in marble stairs and wrought iron railings, in flooding *fondamenti* and creaking wooden bridges. The Rialto and Accademia stand as quiet witnesses to the hijinks and carousing in the streets around them. From above the Grand Canal in the moonlight, you can barely discern the silhouettes of late-night partygoers forced to squat contributions at the end of a wooden pier, their identities cloaked.

As in all dreams, Venezia holds these moments as hidden pockets of honey, difficult to separate from fantasy. Quiet footfalls become a gentle clop of hooves on stone while old gates swing open like there's someone home. Gilded *carnivale* masks laugh from darkened store shelves. Worn brass door knockers rage mutely as you stop to finger the deep impressions of a long-gone ghetto gate that once barred all of the city's Jewry.

Such sights melt away as the frozen tang of *sgroppino* slips down your throat. It's a perfect lemon dreamsicle with hints of champagne that sweetly balances the burn of cigarette smoke in your throat. Your head spins pleasantly, it's been so long.

Finally, warm shoulders of friends carry you home—hands, legs, and arms entwine and release—as you close the distance with revived soles. Time to say goodnight, pausing to press cheeks before sliding under crisp, cool covers starched like soldiers.

Venezia is a dream, indeed; perhaps unfulfilled so that you can return to it again—always, forever—in your mind.

3 Setembre: Serendipity in the City

Serendipity finds its way though cities in a never-ending ribbon of surprises. For instance, one would never expect to meet a familiar face after *l'uno* in Campo S. Stefano, but it can happen if stars are aligned.

On our last night in Venezia, as Iole and I stepped arm in arm back to the Hotel Ca' San Marcuola, we passed a dark-haired man who gave us a double-take and a wide grin. Walking home from work, Denis greeted us with cheek kisses and easily swept us in the opposite direction for farewell drinks.

After the bar closed, we meandered through the dark alleys, gently lamplit in yellow pools, surrounded by a familiar sense of quiet enchantment. There's another Venezia underneath the one who presents herself during the day; at night, one finds pockets of life everywhere—under bridges, in alleys, beneath arches, flowing through the canals, and in small plazas where people smoke pot and drink wine from plastic cups.

Relishing the secret flavor of this last mission, our voices joined others that reverberated off the walls, growing louder and softer as we night owls passed each other briefly before continuing on, turning right and left in a great labyrinth.

Like the first night we spent together, Iole, Denis, and I shared drinks and cigarettes freely between us. As I held a mouthful of cool, light Italian beer before swallowing it, topics that I have not yet covered in Civita began to play in my mind: I realized that Iole and I were witnessing the interaction of hidden spaces, serendipity, and chance.

…Were it not for a mention from Bonnie last summer, I would not have known of NIAUSI nor applied for this fellowship.

…Were it not for this fellowship journey to Civita, I never would have met Iole.

…Were it not for Iole's companionship, I would not have traveled from Civita to Venezia for the Biennale.

…Were it not for a teaching position in Venezia this summer, Iole would not have visited the same bar for her nightly *sgroppino* (lemon gelato, vodka, prosecco) and met Klevis and Denis, who served her.

…Were it not for Klevis and Denis, we would have missed out on a marvelous Never-Never-Land adventure.

The night we arrived, neither Denis nor Klevis were at work; instead, they were at dinner, as Klevis was recuperating from a broken tooth, the result of a punch from an intoxicated tourist. When Klevis learned that Iole had returned to Venezia, he invited us to join them for a meal that set the rest of our escapade in motion.

Dinner and several pitchers of *vino rosso della casa* at Pier Dickens in the Dorsoduro Sestiere were followed by a deliciously long walk to the Cannaregio Sestiere, the location of our hotel. Our trek was encumbered by Signor Rossi, Iole's impossibly heavy red rolling suitcase, which earned its name after Denis asked what was inside, and I said that we were carrying a man's body.

Up small bridges and down flights of stairs, Klevis and Denis took turns managing Signor Rossi, whose wheels made loud noises on the stone streets. As we walked, Iole gave us the history of several buildings; when we passed an open bar, we stopped for drinks, laughing and telling stories in a rapid mixture of English and Italian. Venezia had become our own private adventure.

Carabinieri strolled past as the guys commandeered several chairs that were locked together in order for us to enjoy our beers and cigarettes in a small *campo* close to the Rialto. It felt like we had a limitless evening to discover the city, yet underneath we knew that we were on borrowed time.

We paused for a drink at Denis' jaw-dropping top-floor apartment *vicino* the Rialto Bridge overlooking the Grand Canal, which imbued us with enough strength to finish the walk home after 3:00 *ore*. Denis and Klevis wouldn't let us go it alone—especially with the corpulent Senior Rossi in tow—so we set out *insieme*, talking about our lives and bumping into each other in a friendly way, not quite believing how much fun we were having as we navigated through the dark city, high on adventure and possibility.

Tonight, Iole and I felt a revival of that exhilaration as we said goodbye to Denis in the wee hours of the morning. It wasn't the same without Klevis, but there was still a bit of magic in our meeting. Upon reaching the campo near Denis' house, we hugged him and kissed his cheeks, sad to see the chapter end.

Now just two, Iole and I sighed our way back to the Cannaregio, feeling the impending end of our adventure as we paused to photograph ourselves at the railing of the Rialto. Arm in arm again, we reveled at our luck of meeting Denis by chance—and the fun of our whole adventure together. We softly agreed at how difficult it would be to return to the world—after all, when one knows that places like Venezia or Civita exist, how can there be anything else?

Even after a five-hour train ride back to Civita in the afternoon, I still didn't have an answer. Instead, I chose to remember the warm echo of our collective laughter on old stone arches and the sweet way we fell into each other as we walked, sparks flying. I thought, too, of Denis taking my hand before we separated and giving it a squeeze, fingers pulling together just as we three pulled apart.

As I passed through the Porta S. Maria gate in Civita—with a much lighter Signorina Violetta rolling behind me on the cobblestones—I also thought of how serendipitous it would be to meet again.

5 Settembre: Bridges to Cross

"The current moment has no idea how to negotiate the coexistence of radical change and radical stasis that is our future."

Five days ago, I recorded that quote while exploring OMA's exhibit on architectural preservation at the Biennale. Sadly for me, Venezia is already on its way to assuming a dream-like status, it seems so long ago. Time bends strangely: one minute stretches on for weeks or even a lifetime in Civita, whereas days begin to dissipate in a few hours once you get outside.

Upon leaving Il Nuovo for mass this morning, Tony and I were swallowed in such a deluge of pushy tourists and their unruly children—and dogs—that I wondered if I wasn't still in Venezia. The weather grows more temperate each day, and school is about to begin; naturally, weekends are perfect for family day trips to dreamy locales.

There are indeed many such dream-like qualities shared by Civita and Venezia: picturesque, pedestrian-only cities whose authenticity has worn with time—and their dependence on tourism; their connectedness (and distance) formed by long man-made bridges; an otherworldly, remote spirit enhanced by very private resident populations; and tenuous supportive structures that either threaten to flood and sink, or erode and disintegrate into the depths below.

In effect, Venezia and Civita are two points of a similar spectrum connected by a road. I don't find it inconsequential that my journey so far has consisted of two dreamlike places where the outside world carries little weight, and where one's focus is continually encouraged inward.

Even in cosmopolitan Venezia, host of the Biennale and the Venice film festival, the best times are to be had discovering secret places in the dark where there are no films, no exhibits, no red carpets.

With such focus, I return to the dilemma of that opening quote: how is it possible to reconcile the static past with the ever-changing future and still remain cohesive? If you aren't who you were, and your identity is always evolving, who are you in the present moment? How does one preserve the past and build toward the future without losing either in the process? Is any identity ever valid if it doesn't last?

I ask myself these questions every day now. How is living in Civita—as a foreigner, not merely a tourist, in a strange land—changing the way I experience life? Who was I when I left, and who will I be when I return? Is one sense of self more valid—out with the old and in with the new?

People and cities share that struggle. If they refuse to adapt and change, they stagnate and decline; yet, when we evolve, we grow out of—and can forget—the rich, evolutionary layering that defines our very existence.

Some believe that the further we walk from our "true" past, especially in terms of cities, the more homogeneous we become: muddled, tasteless, and lacking in strong character or historical foundation.

Yet, if the very nature of time is to move and shift, then why bother struggling to preserve anything? A passage from Italo Calvino's "Invisible Cities" comes to mind:

> *"Sometimes different cities follow one another on the same site and under the same name, born and dying without knowing one another, without communication amongst themselves. It is pointless to ask whether the new ones are better or worse than the old, since there is no connection between them, just as the old postcards do not depict Maurilia as it was, but a different city which, by chance, was called Maurilia like this one."*

When I reflect on what Venezia and Civita were—and are—perhaps the only answer for any of us is to transform with wisdom, knowing that the bridge between what was and what is simply grows longer rather than falling into ruin behind us.

Rather than wholesale renovation or change, perhaps the point is find ways of tapping into an original potent identity in order to inform the layers of an ever-changing future—with intelligence, poetry, and authenticity.

Thankfully, Civita and Venezia are parts of that bridge for me, which makes the span between the world that came before I arrived and the one I create today quite desirable to cross again and again.

The Witching Hour

The laden clunk of the tumbler *aperta la porta* to a once familiar scene, now cloaked in inky night with glowing orbs of sulphur in between. In the dark, every sound reports like a cannon: the scrape of sandals on stone echo like insults to the evening's peace.

Ancient homes disappear down dead-end alleys, and the valley below is lost except for static penlights like fireflies caught—immobile—in jars. Stillness sets as no stillness does at day; no wind to blow, no churching bells to pray. *Il capo gatto*, Nerone, oily black and languid, brushes past my calf as he slinks to the *piazza*, blending into buildings and shadow to join *la festa* where all *gatti* come to play.

Owls break treaty with searching calls for prey, accompanied by the noxious click of nighttime *insetti*, thousands of legs stroking tinny, overstressed strings—an ensemble *senza maestro*. To wander in their music is to hear beetles skitter and the reproachful scratch of leaves against each other, a chorus of brittle fingernails on stone. In the orchestra pit, a praying mantis cinched in high-collared green vestments squares off with a treacherously patient spider who has set his hundred eyes on something fat and juicy in between.

Midnight in paradise, a spell that keeps the curious awake, I'm equally clothed in darkness so as not to offend or distract or pierce in any way. The muted notes of a woman's aria call to me from behind a window where the silhouette of a man moves in the light. From his chimney curls the aroma of fired bread; through his door, the sound of an unseen glass refilled.

Perhaps the haunted dreams of every Civitonici collect here in shadows where *giardini* grow black and holes are endless; where unsteady feet trip on uneven stones. *La luna* winks shyly from behind her filmy negligee of haze, half as full as she'll be as we approach the harvest days. Fall's crisp air settles down, layer upon layer, building a foggy comforter of clouds that buffers us as we sleep. As the houses settle, the stone and wood creak, like buildings dreaming the dreams of those inside.

No flies, no mosquitoes, no tourists, no planes, no bells, no tractors, no scooters, no festivals, no masses, no tables, no chairs, no plates, no tablecloths. No gate too high, no stone too cold, no street deserted so long as I walk there. There is only adventurous anonymity, a string of lamplights that bow in yolky haloes, and my eyes, which search to make sense and remember the secret shades of the witching hour in Civita.

Six

"Can we reconcile the ever-static past with the ever-changing future and still remain cohesive?"

11 Settembre: Possession

When discussing age in Italian, I find it amusing that one "has" years. *Per esempio, in italiano*, I would say, *"Io ho trenta sei anni."* The notion of possessing one's age is pleasing, as if it's possible to hold time: I hold 36 years and I own every one of those damned minutes.

It's equally amusing how many times I've been asked my age here. It's impossible to tell what motivates this question; pure curiosity, to see if the veneer matches the number of rings? Or, do I appear markedly young (or old) in comparison with how I present myself?

We held a contest at dinner on Thursday after Marco inquired this of me, and the table's conversation immediately hushed with interest. I suggested that someone guess before I revealed the answer. Nina was close with 32 *(che carina!)*, however—*naturalamente*—it's no surprise that this question arose again a day later.

After scaling a gate leading into the *giardino* at the farthest reach of Civita before the road veers right toward Mary of the Incarcerated, Fabrizio popped that question in frustration at my resistance to his advances. "Gabriela," he demanded, *"quanti anni hai?"*

We were mid-caper, standing in the darkness at midnight in the backyard of a *palazzo* owned by wealthy Romans. Behind me stood dramatically lit buildings with grand ionic columns, as if Caesar himself stayed over occasionally. Down below, the valley was cloaked in deepening shades of pitch, alit only with small clusters of lamps, including ones that brightened Fabrizio's *agriturismo*.

When I said that I was 36, he gestured emphatically, like I had given him the ammunition he sought. *"Tu hai trenta sei anni; io ho trenta sette anni; siamo in Civita—paradiso—non vuoi avventura? Romanza?"* With the right person, that question is easy to answer. Romance and adventure in an ancient town with old stone streets, delicious wine and food, and gentle yellow lamplight? *Si, certamente!*

I winced, realizing that I had allowed my eagerness for exploration and the makings of a good story to place me in circumstances where I shouldn't be. When he met me coming out of Tony's after dinner, wanting to share a glass of *vino rosso* at his father's house, I thought it might go toward a sense of goodwill...and I was interested in seeing places that are perpetually locked to everyone.

We drank Fabrizio's wine and a splash of Vin Santo inside Felice's rustic quarters, the place that held a curious late-night party a week ago. Then, he led me on a tour through the closed *bruschetteria* where we shared a draught of homemade *limoncello* and a rare opportunity to push the olive press—the 1,500-year-old stone wheel press that bears the sign, "Do Not Touch!" He showed me how they once crushed the olives, filtered them in woven baskets, then pressed the oil with a giant metal contraption.

Inside the *bruschetteria* hang things beyond imagining: old iron tools, grappling hooks, and harnesses for beasts of burden that walked in a circle to move the press, all situated around a well that dips so deep into Civita's stone that it's possible to smell water even today.

Fabrizio hopped back and forth, showing me a series of alabaster cones that fit inside one another to collect rainwater, which was then used for cooking and washing. Every artifact was a treasure as much as the exposed stone structure itself, so naturally, this was the point where I began to kick myself for not bringing *la mia macchina fotografica*.

We stepped next door from the *bruschetteria* to tour one of his family's homes, which I've walked past hundreds of times, but assumed was used for storage. A modest old wooden door with a lock, I never imagined that this is where his *nonni* once lived—and he occasionally haunts.

He showed me the old stove where Vittoria cooked for him as a child, and the dining room where a mural of Civita is painted on one wall and dusty photos and tattered banners hang from the other, evidence of past-gone glory. He showed me a more recent photo of him and his daughter, Chiara, winning a donkey race when she was a toddler—the same race that will take place here tomorrow.

It was exhilarating to continue this secret exploration. From the ancient olive press to generations of family relics and forgotten rooms, we then clambered into a forbidden garden, guarded by a threatening gate topped with sharp metal spears. Fabrizio climbed over as if it were nothing, placing his hands over the spears as I scaled it next, tentative in every step. Looking out from the edge of the cliff, he turned me around to kiss me as I pushed him away several times, finally uttering, *"Basta! Siamo amici! Solamente amici!"*

He continued to impress upon me his argument, "Gabriela, *tu sei bellissima—bella, bella, bella. Ti desidero. Perchè no?*" I spoke again of friendship, to which he responded that, in Italy, it's impossible to be only friends with a beautiful woman whom one desires.

We climbed back over the gate onto the *decumanus maximus* in disagreement, parting ways at Felice's house where he was staying for the evening. He encircled my waist, pulling me to him, against which I raised my hands to his chest. *"Basta. Siamo amici,"* I said, placing my hands down against him emphatically with my words. He dropped his hands, commenting on how Americans are so closed, tight, *senza avventura.*

"Non è vero! Non sono!" I gestured at myself with defiance. He sighed and shook his head, leaning up against the stone building, saying that he didn't understand. I paused, then called, *"Ci vediamo,"* as I turned to leave.

He snorted and said in Italian, "Of course. I live here. Where do you live?" It pleased me that my immediate answer was, *"Abito qua!"*

He shook his head and responded, *"No, non abiti qua—tu abiti a Seattle."*

That statement played in my mind as I drifted off to sleep against the howling wind, a raging daylong tempest that still whistled through the hearth and rattled the outer doors. Seattle, Civita—where do I live now? A person who looks like me will return to the Pacific Northwest in October, but she won't be the same person who left.

Exploring this paradise, as Fabrizio called it—filled with angels and imps, fire and dance, bridges and bluffs, stones and gardens—is surely transforming me. Yet, as I hold each of these days and nights, and the minutes in between, I will always remain in possession of myself.

Whomever I turn out to be.

30 Settembre: Nature, Nurture and Civita

In the debate over which impresses more influence—Nature or nurture—I've historically believed that it's more Nature, due to my own circumstances.

Today, I considered the fact that families, with their complicated network of relationships and hidden caverns pregnant with emotional cobwebs, are in many ways not so different in structure from Civita. From the outside, things appear peaceful, even inactive; underneath, there are ancient tears into the bedrock that will never be healed.

Jerry, Ron, and I investigated similar gouges in the stone caves underneath one of Felice and Margarita's properties, which hold ancient olive oil pressing rooms and caves for storing and aging meat. With eerily familiar hopping footsteps, Fabrizio's father, Felice, walked us through the olive press room, as if he was on camera. There was something in his short, paunchy balding stature, his showy yet furtive movements, that recalled the form and gait of Fabrizio—and the question of Nature and nurture.

Looking closer at Felice, I can now see all of him in Fabrizio's face, stature, and the animation of his limbs. Both are older brothers. Both have a love of Civita and a tie to the land, especially Fabrizio with his gift for making olive oil and wine. I couldn't help but wonder how much of this he learned at his father's knee—or at his *nonna*, Vittoria's, stove—and how much of this was simply born into his bones, a mitochondrial legacy that he could not refuse?

Later, as we took a walk towards the tunnel that runs underneath Civita, Jerry suggested that we stop by Antonio's garden, which was when I learned how much of Civita that Antonio and Rossana actually own. We stepped though an old wooden gate secured with a rusty bar to find a series of caves that I had never seen before, including one that appeared to lead deep into Civita's main bedrock.

I also discovered the reason that I see Antonio on the back road so often when I'm perched on my writing rock: he's raising chickens in the shallower caves! (When informed of this, Tony sniffed dryly, much to my amusement and said, "Well, of course he's got chickens back there. He's always had chickens.")

After bidding hello to the hens, we walked through the tunnel and down into the chestnut groves. There, we dodged large fuzzy seed pods that fell at regular intervals from the trees, as if propelled by an army of angry squirrels. On the way back up, we stopped to pick up old relics on the path—broken pottery, a piece of tufa connected with carved basalt, probably part of a doorway—and I wondered if any of those pieces belong to the houses I've come to know, and who might have lived there that I'll never meet.

Domenica and Mario, Vittoria and Luigi, Rossana and Antonio, Antonella and Elena—I'm becoming more aware of the many families who lived long before my arrival. I'm also sensing that we are at an intermission; the grown-up children are just beginning to have their babies, and it will be 10 to 20 years before those children are old enough to unite with any semblance of the same force that thrived in their grandparents' and great-grandparents' generations.

Something similar is true of NIAUSI (from the viewpoint currently afforded me.) From Jerry, I hear of the high days of students pouring into Civita, Astra's didactic dinners, project presentations in the *palazzo*, and secret explorations that involved crawling on one's belly with candles into claustrophobic spaces to find caves lined with Etruscan tiles. While an occasional forbidden garden exploration might occur these days, I sense that the next wave of activity has yet to happen—and may be several years away. NIAUSI and its Fellows are in another adolescence, or perhaps a mid-life transition.

Later, I brought Jerry and Ron to Massimo's Bar to inquire about a man that they took a photo of in 2007. For three days, they have searched Bagnoregio for this guy, likely in his 80s, who drives a scooter with a windshield held together by duct tape. No one else could identify him, but I had a feeling that Massimo would know. Naturally, he took one look at the grinning, wrinkly man in the photo and rattled off his name and address.

As we enjoyed our Campari sodas, I asked Massimo, *"Di dove sei? Bagnoregio?"* He told me that his mother actually came from Civita—she lived in a home on Via Mercatello—and his father came from Bagnoregio, mere feet away. They once owned a *pizzeria* where all of the local agricultural college students came, and now they own only the bar.

As we sat in Massimo's chairs *davanti al PT,* I felt daunted—especially as I heard Jerry's colorful stories about how many different ways he has explored Civita and all of the people he formed relationships with, some of whom are already dead. Had I come to Civita too late?

I've missed knowing Astra and so many of the important Civitonici who are permanently gone; I've missed the restoration that's happened over many years; I've missed being part of the student brigade who stormed Civita, and for those things I haven't missed, I'm quite far behind so many others in their time and relationships here.

Then, I took a different view, as I began to envision a network with tendrils stringing from these past memories (which must be recorded and safeguarded) into a very dense tapestry that stretches into the future. One where people like Iole, Jonathan, Helen, and I return to Civita to see Elena and Alberto grow up, to see the food institute become a reality—accompanied by a NIAUSI café, of course—and a strong contingent of Fellows, interns, and members who faithfully return in overlapping months, years, and specialties to help fortify Civita's future and become part of this ancient family.

When I return to my original question, the more strongly I concur that it is Nature that ultimately governs us. We can learn and unlearn a million nurtured things in a lifetime; and, in fact, how we nurture ourselves is an act of sheer will.

But Nature is the true divining force; if not, then how else can one explain the magnetic draw that those of us called here experience—as if our cells and our hearts know from whence they come, and when they've finally find their way home?

9 Settembre: Time and Trust

A week in Civita without the people I quickly came to love in August has rendered me—and the town—markedly silent. I miss the ongoing *chiacchierare alla piazza* between Josè, Gaia, Maria, and Marcella, without whom my Italian education is suffering. Within this vacuum of activity, I'm finally beginning to understand the threatening serenity that hangs over this place.

Despite ominous thunderheads this morning, the need for exercise overcame me, so I ventured out of Il Nuovo without knowing how far I dared to go, armed only with my notebook and camera. Optimistic about my chances of staying dry, I continued out the main gate, headed for Bagnoregio. As I neared the staircase that leads to the belvedere, a gray, creeping shape caught my attention: *un piccolo gattino* walking along the busy switch-back road.

To date, my luck with Civita's cats in general (and Betty's kitten, *Due Mila Diece*, specifically) has been slim, save for love from *il mio fidanzato*, Nerone. After Betty and DMD scampered away—again—the other night, Tony reminded me that it takes time (and often food) to build trust, so I was surprised when this little one didn't skitter off, but actually began to follow my soothing words.

The scant puffball mewed pathetically when we reached the base of the stairs, tugging hard on my heart strings, so I was determined to shepherd it toward the café at the top of the bluff. Without money to buy food, I figured there had to be a scrap of discarded treat up there; in any case, I felt compelled to deliver it away from the street where it was sure to become road kill for the white bus to Bagnoregio.

Who knows why the little guy trusted me, or how it even understood what to do (Nature versus nurture?), but that kitten hauled itself up five flights of stairs, following the sound of my footsteps and gentle prodding in Italian.

When we reached the top, some German tourists scared it by stepping too quickly; I nearly left before I realized that it was stumbling around looking for me, rather than trying to escape. I called to it and it came running, an awkward toddler still finding its gait. It didn't have its full sense of sight, it was so young.

Smart thing, it crept around the café looking for food, which is where I left it, hearing it mew in the distance as I continued on after several minutes. What else to do? My heart sank as I sat near the statue of S. Bonaventura, wondering if the kitten would be okay. Tony already has six cats, so there was no bringing it home, if it would even follow me or let me carry it all the way back to Civita—which is home to many hungry cats anyway.

With a sniff, I thought about that layering of cats in Civita, perhaps the longest contiguous resident group in town. It scares me to think that the children and grandchildren who will ultimately inherit this place may not understand what they're receiving or won't make it a priority to visit longer than a few weeks a year: Alessandra's boys, Ludivico and Giovanni; Marco and Inga's children, Niko and Nina; Fabrizio's daughter, Chiara; Gaia and Bernardo's grandchildren, Emma and Thomas. The others have adult children who rarely, if ever, visit this place.

The main challenge to Civita's social continuity is the one short month that most residents (or NIAUSI Fellows) remain. These vacationers come and go, but those who keep Civita running are a different group, more insular, and even they are not all full-time residents; most live in Bagnoregio. How, then, do places like Civita hope to maintain a legacy of memory and a living soul if there aren't year-round families to carry that torch?

The clouds darkened, so I retraced my steps to Civita, taking the belvedere path in hopes of spotting the *gattino*. To my delight, a woman scooped it up in her arms just as I neared the café, cooing as all Italians do when they encounter a baby of any kind, *"Che carino!! Vedi, un bambino!"* as she nestled the kitten into the crook of her arm. Her husband searched their car for food and I allowed myself to believe that the case was closed: I fulfilled my duty by moving the kitten to a safe place where it could be adopted.

On my way back to Il Nuovo, I smiled at Ivana, who owns the gift shop under which she lives, and waved over at Emanuela, taking a break from the kitchen at the *osteria*, her hands on her hips. Passing me on the way to her family's *bruschetteria*, Antonella gave me a nod and a, *"Buon giorno,"* while Antonio waved down and smiled from the top of the stairs, surveying his lunch crowd.

Like Betty's kitten, who continues to give me a distant once-over, the behind-the-scenes folks have been doing the same throughout town. They may not all be residents, but they keep Civita running, day in and day out—Sandro with his tractor, Anna Rita in the church gift shop, Antonio, Antonella, Emanuela, Ivana, Raphaele, and many others.

I've come to see the similarity between the instant trust that the kitten placed in me and how quickly the first group of Civitonici befriended me. Like the *gattino* on the road, I see what we all have in common: Civita is part of our journey, but it's not our year-round home.

In transitory settings where we're all equally "in between," there is less to lose; it's easier to be more open to strangers when you are a stranger yourself.

Seven

"we all have an effect on each other, a layering of influence over time."

21 Agosto: making good choices

Laying in bed as the sun rose this morning, I reflected on design as a series of good choices. For example, an architect can choose to orient a building so as to minimize its heat gain and maximize its alignment with wind patterns for natural ventilation. If that's not possible, then the designer can choose to mitigate the effects of what she cannot change.

Civita presents constrained choices: limited land, topographic challenges, erosion, and exposure to the elements. Yet, simple design solutions made thousands of years before "green building" have produced extremely comfortable outdoor spaces and buildings that don't require mechanical equipment.

Civita's green walls and pocket gardens not only provide food and tranquil outdoor living rooms, they lessen the heat island effect. (In the U.S., we excitedly label a mid-rise condo "sustainable" if it has a ivy trellis.) For buildings that cannot avoid heat gain, such as Il Nuovo, which rises tall to confront the sun, windows are equipped with interior wood shutters that can be closed to block out the heat.

The more I continue to pull apart the thoughtfulness of the design choices surrounding me in Civita, the more I find that it's quite a bit like the choices one is faced with in life.

Yesterday, upon returning home from shopping, I heard a man call my name, seemingly from the courtyard below. When I looked out the window and saw no one, I realized that he was

actually calling from inside Lo Studio, the other NIAUSI home connected to mine. *"Permesso?"* he called.

My heart raced; I couldn't imagine how someone had been able to enter my home. I wondered if I was in danger, realizing later that this was the first time I felt threatened during the entire trip.

As he stepped into the dim light of the interior stairs, I saw that it was Fabrizio, which didn't make me feel any more safe. "Gabriela...*permesso?*" he asked, slowly ascending the stairs step by step. I could see that he was attempting not to spook me, but his measured footsteps actually made me feel as if I were being hunted and cornered.

With a wine bottle in my hand, I realized that I had a weapon if I needed it. My heart thudded in my ears as I struggled to ask in Italian how he managed to be inside. Turns out, the door to Lo Studio was never locked after Jonathan the intern left. I had been vulnerable this whole time.

He continued slowly toward me up the stairs, suggesting in Italian that we have a glass of wine together. With the shutters closed to keep out the heat, Il Nuovo was suddenly a very dark, small place.

I moved quickly away through the interior double doors into the kitchen to set my bags down, but Fabrizio followed me saying, *"Permesso? ...Ach,* Gabriela, *sei bella, bella,"* reaching out to gently touch the side of my face.

It was hard to conjugate words correctly as I skirted past him from the kitchen back out to the vestibule, my hands shaking. In measured words, I said, *"Se vuoi il vino, dobbiamo andare alla piazza,"* holding my hands up to stop him from coming closer. He explained that he couldn't go to the *piazza* because his daughter was at Tony's speaking on Skype with her mother; he pressed me again to share a glass of wine together in my home.

"No, non è possibile," I said, hearing my voice become strained. When he asked why we couldn't have wine together in my house, I responded with distress, *"Non conosco te!"*—I don't know you!

With exasperation, he responded, *"Ach! Ecco me...Fabrizio!"* and some assurance that he had no intention of hurting me. In a burst, I grabbed my purse and keys and moved us both out the front door, locking Il Nuovo behind me.

He asked where I was going; the only good choice I could see was a populated place. *"Devo lavorare; io vado alla piazza."* I told him that I needed to work, and that I was going to the *piazza.* My hands trembled minutes later as I sat on the stone bench.

Later that evening, Tony and I enjoyed red wine and our latest creation, baked potato torte layered with zucchini, ham, cheese, and onion, topped with zucchini flowers. Fabrizio then came to make his case in the proper way.

Tony sat at the head of the long table, and Fabrizio, dressed up in black, brought a chair to sit opposite me. I felt like we were actors in an adult version of a TV show where the teenage suitor

— 63 —

asks the girl's father if it's okay to take her out on a date. For much of the conversation, in between winks whenever I met his eyes, Fabrizio and I spoke through Tony, each of us asking him, *"Come si dice...?"*

When Tony left the table, Fabrizio asked if I'd like to join him for dinner at his house sometime. At that moment, I began to understand the nature of his desire and his boldness, which was akin to the way Giovanni and Ludivico pressed Alessandra with their antics. When they really want something, boys of any age will continue pushing to get it, no matter how often they are told, "No."

In considering choices, I could also see the constraints in Fabrizio's world: hands-on management of an *agriturismo*; divorced father of a young girl who lives most of the year with her mother in the U.S.; embedded in small-town life where the residents don't change and the visitors don't stay.

But, I had to trust my gut, so I thanked him and politely declined. He left soon after, and this time, I think he understood.

In spite of everything, I felt a little bad for him, but then I reminded myself that in order to design a sustainable life, one must learn to make good choices early on—and find ways to lessen the adverse effects of the things one cannot change.

6 Settembre: From Darkness, Light

It's not obvious that a tunnel runs underneath Civita. As with most of life's discoveries, there are no helpful signs directing you past the edge of town to locate this secret treasure. To find it, you must intuit that there may be a reason to keep walking as the street dips to the right, turning from orderly stones to dirt.

If you continue on, you'll pass man-made caverns, likely used for storage when they were carved as they are today. You'll also find a shrine dedicated to Mary of the Incarcerated, which she certainly is. To the right of her barred cell is a slit where visitors may leave offerings—like the opening where a prisoner receives food—Mary's (and Mother Church's) daily bread.

The image of Mary imprisoned gives a clue to the emotional tone of this face of Civita. Even with the bustle of tourists above, this path becomes desolate quickly, as most merely pause to snap a photo of the valley before heading back on the *decumanus maximus* for lunch at Antonio's *bruschetteria*.

The view from this side of Civita is very different looking up; it's possible to see the craggy drops at the back of people's yards, which once continued further out before landslides and erosion ate away the edges of town. Here, the only sound, besides a gentle breeze in your ears, is the annoying buzz of black flies like the ones at Luca's house. They press persistently in your face as you push through high weeds, relentless as if to deter explorers from venturing forward.

It feels as though you shouldn't visit this place, it's so still. On the right are inlets into Civita's old caves, now boarded or chained closed. This walk reminds me of the old Roman myths where seekers descended into the Underworld to find treasure or rescue a lost lover.

Brushing past dead trees, the mouth of the tunnel finally comes into view; my hands trembled uncontrollably as I stepped closer, foot by foot. A light shone at the end of the tunnel—it wasn't long—but it was dark in the middle. I took it as a good sign that butterflies flitted about the entrance; yet, as I stepped inside, I fought images of horror films. "Don't go in there alone!" I could hear myself shrieking to the heroine, as she entered the spooky cave by herself.

My hands shook the camera, making several blurry photos, as my imagination conjured spiders and bats, (or worse—large rats, like the ones we saw in Venezia) scuttling about me. I stopped in the middle to take a breath; the only sound was the crunch of dead leaves and gravel under my sneakers. My pace quickened at the end where I could see enough to avoid leftover beer bottles from some late-night party.

As I turned around to look at the tunnel from the other side, I pictured it during a different time when it was constantly in use: people passing one another to transport goods to the next town or storing their wares in one of the underground caves. Not so scary, right?

I stepped further into the light, unnerved by the sheer drop to the valley floor on the right, which pricked my fear of heights, but not enough to stop my appreciation of the beautiful trees and the view across to Lubriano.

My return journey was different; from the other end, the light spread farther into the cave, allowing me to discern more inlets, each blocked by cascades of small rocks. Arriving back in Civita's upper world, I thought about the concept of tunnels, which denote hiding or secrecy, places where things or people are buried, a sense of covert acts. They are places in which things gestate—beings that don't need or are repelled by light, justice, or truth.

Tunnels can hold things that we fear; in dreams, they can represent a connection with our darker side, the place where our unconscious desires writhe unchecked.

Yet, tunnels also help us see the center of solid or seemingly impenetrable things; in tunnels we can discern a series of strata that are not visible from the outside. They not only convey us through those layers, they serve to transport us—to take us from one side to the other and enable us to perceive a different perspective upon reaching the other side.

Compared to bridges, which can be seen by the laziest eye, it's compelling to consider what it means to move through a hidden conveyance, be it a tunnel, a great endeavor, or a rite of passage. For thousands of years we have continued to step towards the light in order to discover new places, even if we could not initially envision them.

Upon exiting the tunnel, I felt changed by my experience of Civita from underneath, though my hands still trembled. As two butterflies ascended from behind me, I realized that it's our human sense of adventure, courage and patience—and faith that there is something worth walking towards—that allows us to emerge, albeit slowly at times, from darkness.

17 Settembre: Embracing Trouble in Paradise

As I begin to share *questo bel paradiso,* as Fabrizio referred to Civita, with my new housemate, I'm finding that my focus has begun to shift. *Veramente,* I am surprised at how much fun I've had sharing my experience in Civita with Helen, whose thoughtfulness, sense of adventure, and curiosity mirror my own. Watching her discover this place has allowed me to experience Civita in new ways.

In the morning, shopping and chit-chit in *italiano* at the Mancini sisters' alimentary, then *caffè e cornetti cioccolati insieme al bar;* in the evening, cooking at Tony's with Lazio veggies from Maria Grazia's small *negozio di verdure.*

During our Bagnoregio trek today, the wind picked up, blustering like a tropical storm (Tony *ha detto* that this weekend's *tempesta* is coming from Africa.) Normally, I hate the wind; *invece,* in Civita, it turns out that many of my tastes are different. Here, I find the wind a wild but welcome experience: racously disheveling one's hair and massaging the skin in waves as the sun shines above the passing *nuvole.*

Thinking back to what Fabrizio said—about this place being an adventure, a paradise, a dream—coupled with the spurring effect of the wind, which swells in me a welcome but unruly spirit, I am beginning to see how places like Civita encourage a sense of being outside the rules. For me, learning to be outside rules—*la programma,* as he called it today—is an ongoing education.

Last year, during my birthday trip to Kona con *il mio amico,* Brad, we came upon a gate with a "No Trespassing" sign at the beginning of our jungle hike in Waimea. When I pointed this out, Brad laughed and said, "Gabbi...seriously. We're in Hawaii." We scaled the fence and found jaw-dropping views that were worth the sweaty 30-minute hike, during which I noted that the guards—who we did indeed meet—had no intention of stopping us. Actually, they waved congenially as they blew past in their jeep.

I balked in similar fashion when Fabrizio suggested that we scale the garden gate to enjoy the view. Naturally, he chided me for my reticence: "Gabriela...*noi siamo a Civita! Loro sono sempre a Roma. Andiamo!*" Learning to possess that kind of mental freedom—not thinking about how to go around, but how to go right over when it's appropriate—is something I continually seek to cultivate—with a dash of sensible restraint and the occasional alley-oop from a partner, of course.

There's something about the power of two. Today, I became aware of how far I've burrowed into a richly solitary life here; so far that I had forgotten the equally savory pleasure of creating shared memories, especially in foreign places.

Call it strength in numbers, perhaps, but it is indeed more fun to share the embrace of wild things—storms, tunnels, gardens, exploring Civita and *la vita bella italiana*—with people like Helen, who see as intently as I do: people who match my courage and desire to delve still deeper together.

Of course, in thinking about paradise, Eden, or perhaps even Civita, we can see that two people left to their own devices can start quite a bit of trouble.

16 settembre: I, Ferry Woman

Earlier today, I riffed on the theme of bridges in my "Letter from Civita" for the NIAUSI fall newsletter. In counting, I realized that people are reading my blog from Washington, California, Oregon, Montana, Massachusetts, Illinois, Florida, and Arizona. Without previously considering the effects of real-time readership, much in the manner of Dickens' serial novels, I realized how important the blog has become to my work. Allowing my readers' commentary to affect me forms a unique and unforeseen bridge of its own.

Knowing that part of my audience is experiencing Civita while I'm here—in real time—has had a deepening effect on my writing and how I experience this place.

As I soaked up the last minutes of late afternoon sun, Antonio stopped to speak with me on his return from taking yet another curious walk down the back side of Civita. With my ever-improving Italian, I was able to discuss my writing and bringing my friends, Kirstin and Sue, to his *bruschetteria* when they visit next week. Not until those words came out in Italian did I feel the wonderful gravity of what their visit means: Sue and Kirstin are my first readers who will experience Civita for themselves.

Minutes later, I met a group of Canadian tourists who ventured past me towards Mary of the Incarcerated. I encouraged them to stop in Maria's *giardino* and recommended that they eat at Trattoria dell'Orso in Orvieto. After we parted company, I realized that I'm no longer a neophyte here; *io sono la scritrice americana*, the American writer perched on her rock.

During yesterday's jaunt to Bagnoregio, I was finally able to explore the *librashop* called Novarea, whose tagline translates to "books and curiosities." During my purchase of an Italian/English version of "Romeo and Juliet," the owner asked me to send her my book when it's finished, something I hadn't dreamed of asking. As Helen and I enjoyed Campari soda at Massimo's Bar, I envisioned my work, *Civita Veritas*, smiling out from Carla Vittoria's shelf, and her *piccolo cane*, Vita, napping in a pool of sunshine behind it.

All at once, it feels like there is momentum behind my life here. Tenuous bridges of serendipity are becoming more stable connections. For a split second, I can picture my friends Tom and Julie arriving next summer, perhaps in time to share figs and prosciutto with Gaia, Bernardo, Ilaria and Marco.

Time and timing are everything. Places like Civita, which is rich in both, use that collective magic to draw people together, if they are open to seeking such things. You can see Civita as a dying castle in the sky, or look deeper to find ancient caves and thousands of insects, tufa stone houses and gardens that feed families, and—of course—people, food, stories, and tradition that alter one's experience of *la vita bella italiana*.

For me, a woman who came here to build new bridges between Civita and the world, those initial foundations and pathways are beginning to take shape through my friends, family, and colleagues. Over the coming weeks, months, and years, it will be a pleasure—and my hope—to watch my two-month adventure continue to ferry new explorers across.

Piano, Piano

So much for drying laundry when the monsoon hits.

In fat droplets, the deluge drives white moths and butterflies from their grapevine shelters like geese to the sky with a gunshot. Oppressive heat, chorused by cicadas, is broken into waves of chords, deep and sonorous and unrelenting, like long, slow bow-strokes of an upright bass.

The percussive spatter peppers blows on the glass until I wonder if the windows will crack. The hasp slips—they blow open—and our conductor, Mother Nature, crashes into the *sala grande* with a cyclone of spray behind her, like Venus on the half shell.

As *la tempesta* strikes, a vaporous relief rises out from the stones—a summertime ghost in search of its bones. From the aroma of warm, wet wood, throaty and rich, emerges a staccato beat as trees drip, drip, drip. The hum of hungry mosquitoes sounds a threatening refrain as Nature unleashes a wind-whipping fury on Civita again.

Thirsty leaves yawn to slurp draughts of rain as the hanging laundry sags on the line, like tired old men in worn undershirts. Their shoulders slumping, they've given up, sinking precariously close to the mud without a care. *Piano, piano,* they release lower still, an orchestra of precariously white sheets in a garden pit of potential ruin.

Across the way, Ludvi brays from Alessandra's balcony; the rain has rudely ended his game. Downstairs, white-haired Maria, forced to abandon her stoop, has shuffled inside—*piano, piano*—her swollen ankles complaining. In a blue smock dress and orthopedic shoes, she sits immediately inside her door, keenly anticipating the moment she can retire outside again, like a triangle player awaiting her only cue.

The wet respite calls the garden turtles to play, slipping deliciously on cool mud and stone while the cats' plans are utterly foiled. Sopranos Massimo and Nerone mewl and complain as they're forced to decamp, driven from bowers of flowers and insulted by damp. Dressed in his tuxedo, Figaro follows them inside, shaking the wetness from his paws in the frantic strokes of a fiddle.

Then—

Piano, piano… The beat turns to tiny tapping, like a drumstick gently on cymbals, and begins to abate. The air lightens, as if Mother Nature has drawn in a breath, and with it, the rank humidity. She taps her baton to call the attention of her players: sun, wind, clouds and rain. A game of musical chairs, they exchange seats, finding there's not room for everyone.

The melody of a calm breeze sweetly coaxes the leaves to flutter and dance, then *piano, piano,* the droplets slow.

And then—silence—they're gone.

Eight

"There are no false moves here, no quick decisions; there's a careful, methodical sense about completing each minute—whether it involves a feet, a conversation, a glass of wine, or a transaction—without rushing to the end."

7 Settembre: Falling is Inevitable

In Civita, autumn is a temptress, slowly drawing warmth from the air. At first, we gladly allow the heat to take its leave—every step falls with less effort, the hills feel less steep, our foreheads less fevered during the climb home. In denial, we insist that summer has weeks more to go; skies are blue, determined tourists continue to trudge through town, and clothes dry quickly on the line.

The dying flit of a brown moth on the windowsill, lacking the strength to escape, tells a different story.

Autumn charms us with her veneer of relief: mesmerizing clouds explode and contract in slow motion, pulling us under the drowsy swell of afternoon naps. No longer crashing like waves, the babbling brook of leaves around Civita's perimeter sings a lullaby from tree to tree, punctuated only by the gentle twitters of small birds returning from vacation in far-off lands.

Standing next to the Marchesa's house, which hangs on a precarious outcropping, it's possible to smell the beginning of harvest in the valley below. The fields may be green, but there is a turning—a fermenting—at work that the nose senses first. When the breeze momentarily regains its strength, warm, smoky draughts from Antonio's *bruschetteria* mix with the fragrant air, and a secret is revealed: fall is stealthily stalking us.

Emanuela agrees, the seasons are changing. A lean, sinewy woman, she sits on the steps outside her Osteria al Forno d'Agnese to down a plate of *bruschetta con pomodori* after the lunch rush subsides.

She personifies that time between summer and fall—the edge of youth set to fade, delayed by a penetrating will of resolve—like those last few hot afternoons in late September when everyone pretends it's possible for summer to last.

Given the option, I'll place my Euros on Emanuela's beauty to last many more rounds; summer is fighting a losing battle and will concede the match long before she does.

For more proof, lean against the edge next to Maria di Venezia's house, which overlooks the remains of the old Roman road. Atop a crumbled stone wall, which quickly falls into nothingness, cling a few straw-colored clumps of dead grasses, telling victims of an expiring season. Down below to the left, a gutted ruin that was once a house blooms wild with verdant trees and vines, but don't be fooled; they're simply the last to go.

My heart leapt to see Gaia and Bernardo's doors and windows open, but it was only their cleaning woman ensuring that all is in its place, which is really what autumn is all about. Fall is meant to fatten us and hold us in the sweetest ways—harvest festivals, fresh nuts, squash vegetables, and wine—until it's too late to outrun winter. She keeps us distracted by brilliant leaves, temperate breezes, and afternoons of long pink light so that we forget the cold, dark months ahead.

To be sure, upon returning home I found Tony cleaning the hearths, moving dustpans of ashes atop piles of dead leaves. The strained light barely filters through the pergola at 17:00 ore, and the sun will disappear behind Il Nuovo soon after. Surprisingly, even flies have little strength to annoy, and the mosquitoes have abandoned their relentless pursuit.

From Oskar's garden, the dying sun shines warm on Lubriano's sand-colored buildings and ginger-toned roofs—a ray of hope—but on my return to *la sala grande*, I notice that Tony's *basilico* is nearly picked clean from last month's culinary endeavors. Seemingly, only Betty's *gattino* is still filled with enough summer optimism to pounce on potential enemies like weeds with any sense of purpose.

A lone minute-man coming to warn us of the impending fall, I watched a grasshopper heave himself inside my kitchen window with his last burst of energy. I could see him respire with labor, the sides of his body moving in and out in gushing breaths.

In…and out; in…and out.

He had lost the green of his brethren who have spent months hopping gleefully between Tony's tomato vines, but I suppose we all lose our bloom with time. I could almost hear him sigh as he leaned against the window frame to expire, mere inches away from the dead moth.

I brightened for a moment when I saw his antennae twitch back and forth, but then I realized that it was only the wind.

13 Settembre: Civita, Christ and a Piazza of Asses

Yesterday, Civita's Piazza S. Donato witnessed an abundance of asses, and this time, I'm not speaking of the tourists. The town held a festival to celebrate the symbol of Christ on the cross followed by several rounds of donkey races around the *piazza*, which drew a crushing crowd of hundreds.

The mood during mass, where we found our pews moved to the right side of *la chiesa* and the center aisle decorated in designs of fresh flowers and leaves, was heightened with energy. Meek Padre Marco was transformed in celebration, draped in a brilliant red stole threaded with gold whorls and crosses; his voice was stronger when he sang, more firm when he spoke. Whether priests or recording artists, when one plays to a packed house, he finds a more ebullient sense of showmanship.

In the early afternoon, Padre Marco and his attendants, including Peppi and Antonio, paraded the large crucifix into the *piazza*, through the main gate, down to Mary of the Incarcerated, and back to *la chiesa* before the donkey races began. A band from Montefiascone entertained us, making me smile to know that all bands know, "Roll Out the Barrel."

As the race set-up commenced, I considered the connection between Civita, Christ, and the ass. Only recently did donkeys stop being a main resource for carrying goods up to Civita; today, we have a sweet man named Sandro who runs goods with his red tractor. If legend is true, Christ was a fan of the donkey, choosing to show solidarity with the common man by riding an ass into Jerusalem rather than a horse. Since this was one of his special feasts, the theme began to make more sense.

Enjoying the first warm sun in days, we watched the riders attempt to mount their donkeys before steering them toward the start line. Enticing them to run forward around the *piazza* several times was another matter. The crowd tittered as at least one donkey per race, if not both, simply refused to cooperate, either running when he should wait or standing still despite sharp spanks from exasperated riders who watched helplessly as their competitors took the lead.

It is exactly this behavior, which presents as stubbornness, that gives the donkey a poor reputation; however, I learned that when donkeys balk they are actually expressing a sense of self-preservation. Donkeys are extremely risk-averse; they listen to an inner sense of boundaries, and when frightened, they elect not to act rashly. Typically, no amount of force or coercion can force their action; they simply must believe that the danger is lifted before they'll comply.

Contrary to popular thought, those who rely on donkeys for labor attest to their dependability, loyalty, and intelligence—once they learn to predict and trust their handlers, which can take years.

Visitors are often greeted by donkeys where their outdoor pens slope up to meet the road to Civita. It's possible to hear them from my bedroom in the morning as they honk at the rising sun like roosters. In fact, they've been a part of this community as long as humans have, which one donkey by the fence reminded me as I walked home after shopping in town.

In 2010, I am my own beast of burden, sweating freely as I carry my groceries in a brown satchel strapped across my chest. Dependable as a donkey, I trek back and forth to Bagnoregio several miles roundtrip every few days to buy food and supplies. (Thankfully, it only involves extra weight on the way home.) Today's journey made me think about the people who live in Civita—reserved, loyal, careful judges of character—and Civita itself: a steady holdout against time, erosion, earthquakes, and landslides.

There are no false moves here, no quick decisions; there's a careful, methodical sense about completing each minute, whether it involves a fest, a conversation, a glass of wine, or a transaction, without rushing to the end. Civitonici weather storms, destruction, and restoration with the same measured patience, quietly refusing to move a minute before they feel sure to do so.

Naturalmente, this means that change and progress—and even decline—happen slowly here, yet I believe this pace of self-preservation is what promotes the endurance of Civita's cultural memory. I've considered that topic from several angles now, and see yet another layer—a bending of time into slower expressions—as actually being helpful to retaining a communal sense of identity.

Residents, workers, and their families absorb the history, meaning, and soul of Civita as they come and go over a lifetime—until they, too, become fully steeped in its flavor like the generations before them. Life in Civita may require more time and dedication, as well as strong legs and lungs, but I don't think that's asinine at all.

4 Ottobre: Just Right

A bad habit resurfaced this morning as I watched Tony catch a lift down to the parking lot with Sandro on his tractor: I gulped my *cappuccino* quickly to catch up with them, though I know that there's time to finish at an appropriate pace and still meet them without delay.

Definitely not *proprio*.

As I tipped my head back in my seat on Piazza Colesanti, Sandro held up his hand and mouthed the words, *"Piano, piano,"* encouraging me to slow down and savor it. Without realizing, I've become distracted by travel arrangements for my trip to Rome, and by decisions that await my attention in Seattle. Last night's insomnia should have been a tip-off, but not until I witnessed Sandro's warning to slow down did I know what was happening.

In Italia, one learns that there is an appropriate setting for everything. Unless it involves driving, time and place typically flow one into another softly and slowly—*piano, piano.* As in Civita, where soil turns into stone, from which raises tufa, which gives rise to gardens, then back to steps and gradually to soil again, one is ensconced in a sense of layered appropriateness and time.

Ironically, as I considered what to leave here metaphorically and what to bring back to Seattle, the essence of expanded time was one concept that I hoped would immigrate. A new definition of home is another that I've been kicking around. While I enjoy Seattle, I feel like Civita has also become a true home to me, though I am not sure yet how to transform that feeling into the appropriate words or a way to stay here longer.

Fabrizio came to chat with me on my rock as I wrote about this yesterday, calling to mind that challenge he put forth a month ago, when I said, *"Ci vediamo,"* and he answered, "Yes, we'll see each other; I live here. Where do you live?" Even then, I instantly said, *"Abito qua,"* and feeling a bit insulted when he shot back, "You don't live here; you live in Seattle."

Abito qua or not, I'm learning that one's sense of belonging is directly tied to a feeling of ownership and involvement, not necessarily how long a person lives somewhere. As I walked home, I heard several Americans capriciously disregard Peppone's widow, Maria, as if she were unintelligent or invisible. (Indeed, she is elderly and doesn't see very well.) They fumbled for her name and the location of the garden in a way that called to mind someone recently dismissing me when she assumed that I didn't speak English. I couldn't help but set them straight as I passed, "Her name isn't Victoria, it's Maria, and the entrance to the garden is that way, through the left."

Seattle is the only other town to which I've felt connected enough to spontaneously offer directions to befuddled tourists, who are usually too distracted with their spread-eagle maps to ask for help. It took me years to get that comfortable, and even then, I rarely feel protective of Seattle like I do of Civita.

Spending two months getting to know this place stone by stone (and there are many more to go) has evoked a unique sense of devotion in me, and an idea for what is *proprio giusto,* or "just right." This experience has also instilled in me a desire for others to approach Civita with a sense of reverence. I make it a point of helping them get it right when they don't know better, if only that they might find something personal here that they can take away, too.

After wiping the *cappuccino* foam off my lips, I rode with Tony into Bagnoregio to say goodbye to the Mancini sisters and Maria Grazia, all of whom showered me with cheek kisses and praises of *carina* and *carissima* as I bade them farewell until next summer. After shopping several times a week with these ladies, getting to know my produce vendors better in Pike Place Market is one habit I'll take back; finding a local butcher and meat and cheese artisans are others.

It should come as no surprise that part of *proprio giusto* and *piano, piano* is taking time to make relationships with the people who feed us—not only to learn about where our food comes from, but to create stronger ties within our own community. It's also about knowing one's neighborhood and the people who live and work there so that we can be a resource to others.

Whether it's knowing the history of a building, the type of fruit hanging on a tree, which alleys interconnect, whose family lives in each house, or the hours that stores are open, learning about a place stone by stone is what makes all the difference in one's experience of it. Becoming observant of people and language, restoration of the church, seasonal food, and investigating the nooks and crannies within Civita is what has informed and transformed my life here.

There's a different experience to be had, for sure. I could live solely by my travel guide, keep a shy distance from the locals, call the place "cute," swig my wine, and leave.

But, as I've slowly learned during my residency, doing so just wouldn't be *proprio giusto.*

19 Settembre: The Value of Time and Tables

One might be tempted to use the well-known phrase, *dolce far niente,* to describe today's events. At 10:45 *ore,* Helen, Tony and I gathered for mass, after which we enjoyed *cappuccini alla piazza insieme* for an hour before we stepped to *pranzare al osteria fino alle 15:00 ore.*

At the table we shared *bruschetta mista (pomodori, cannellini, e due typi di olivi), gnocchi con pomodoro, ravioli con melanzane, e corniglio aceto,* followed by *una torta cioccolata con pere e crema.* We discussed architecture, earthquakes, minimalism, travel, our homes, language, socio-linguistics, the 9/11 memorial, friends in common, plans for our return to Seattle, and—of course—food.

When I returned to Il Nuovo to write notes from my balcony, pausing to appreciate the gentle rain and passing clouds, that phrase, *dolce far niente*—or, "the sweetness of doing nothing"—crossed my mind but I quickly abolished it. I have done nothing before and I find truly doing nothing to be quite boring—unless I'm ravaged by the flu. Our shared table time today was far from *noioso*.

I asked myself, what is the value of time, then? Or, put another way, what is the value of not rushing time? What is the value of human connection without hastening through a meal or mentally moving on to the next thing?

In the States, we use meals to refuel our bodies, often standing while we hold our food in one hand; engineers of "fast food," we don't leave ourselves time to sit and eat, let alone digest. In Italia, lunch and dinner are established pauses for people to enjoy one another. There is sequence and rhythm to the Italian meal, but above all, everything is shared: plates of food, carafes of wine, conversation, and certainly time. We attempt this with "family style" restaurants in the U.S., but it's certainly not for all, especially those who want the freedom of space and separation.

Perhaps that's the real difference: people are more giving of their time and space to one another here. With phrases like, "time is money," perhaps that's why much of the world is so stingy with it. We see long lunches as a time sink (unless we're signing a contract), and we often only make time for long meals—or sit-down dinners—on special occasions rather than as a daily matter of course.

While the Slow Food and Slow Money movements are commendably calling attention to the human need for—and benefit from—the equation I paraphrase as *time + (local) food + connection = happiness + health + (local) wealth,* I wonder how possible it is for the rest of us to embrace and validate such foreign concepts.

The U.S. was populated by Western immigrants who desired space: physical space to homestead outside of crowded cities, political and religious space to worship or support a cause without persecution, the space to say what we think without being executed or jailed—and later, space to drive our single-occupant vehicles. However, by founding a nation on the idea of *space = freedom,* we have nurtured a culture of isolationism. Since such a place had to be built from the ground up, we also birthed the concept of *time = money,* our noses bent ever closer to the grindstone.

Time may be money in a sense, but what my days in Civita continue to confirm—especially at the table—is that time spent together is gold. When we think about "saving up," we should consider the time we spend together as daily savings toward the wealth of our relationships—our emotional bank accounts.

After all, what is the price of our "free time" if it comes at the expense of rich friendships that infuse flavor to the minutes and milestones of our lives? When we reach those later years, which are best shared with lifelong friends, it will be time squandered if life was all about hoarding each second to ourselves—and we'll likely be alone when we polish those pennies.

Of course, what has reinforced that knowledge—and what will shape how I live ever after—are the meals I've shared in Civita and the wealth I continue to discover thanks to the new accounts of friendship I've opened here.

Nine

"Perhaps a couple of passionate women, their heads together in animated conversation, can inspire new growth in Civita — first cabbages, then queens and kings."

15 Settembre: Walk of Fate

Considering how time, serendipity, and personal evolution react with one another, there is one universal truth: until you are ready for particular things to come into your life—relationships, careers, certain vegetables, Hemingway, opera—they can cross your path a thousand times without having any effect.

There are also places in this world like Civita that are rich in after-soul, memory, tradition, and nature, which together perpetually nurture a sense of destiny, attracting those who seek something—oftentimes without even knowing what.

After sharing *cappuccini e cornetti* with my new housemate, Helen, at Peppone's Bar this morning, I realized that, many of us seeking to find ourselves end up in Civita. As Bonnie and Stephen did for me, Helen was introduced to NIAUSI by a friend she met in painting class, who firmly asserted that she must visit Civita during her yearlong sabbatical.

In a short while, Helen and I will venture down to Bagnoregio's *librashop* and Massimo's bar, two new experiences for me. To date, the timing—and the availability of mobile company—has been absent; at 17:00 *ore*, when the book shop opens, I am always mid-essay, and by 19:00, cocktail hour has begun.

Evenings in Civita have historically been a time for sitting in the garden and *chiacchierrare*, followed by wine and dinner *insieme*. When I invited Helen to join me on this adventure, I became aware of the pattern I've created (and deeply enjoy)—as well as my growing desire to venture beyond my small corner of paradise.

To date, I have written about Civita's weather, gardens, festivals and structures, but dawn/day and sunset/night are two concepts that I've consciously saved for when it felt right to explore. Rituals of food and wine, the mountainous topography, and the pure enjoyment of Tony's company have kept my gravity close to home; yet, just as serendipity opened my eyes to another Venezia after dark, I sense that it's time to broaden my experience of Civita—especially after the sun sets.

Like my newfound appreciation of Wagner's "The Ring of Nibelung," (to my delight, Tony played "The Rhine Gold" during last weekend's wild tempest), the timing must be right for certain encounters to have meaning and effect. In considering the coincidence of Helen's arrival just as I'm ready to venture out, I believe that it's the power of Civita, time, and my old friend serendipity that drew us here to find each other in the process of finding ourselves.

Some people are able to accomplish these things in their therapist's office; others of us need to climb a hill or two before we can get there. *Secondo me,* I think it's good to get out once in a while.

21 settembre: Of cabbages and kings

One particular phenomenon has struck me on this trip: the conspicuous social gathering of men. Every day, cliques of six to ten fellows ranging from their 50s to 90s meet in tight circles all across Italy—outside coffee houses, bars, *enoteche,* restaurants, parks—and anywhere that offers plastic red chairs advertising coffee or beer.

No matter where we visit, I find these coteries in impressive numbers—in front of a *pizzeria* in Castiglione in Teverina, outside the movie theater in Bagnoregio, and atop the belvedere in Lubriano. The men past retirement hold court all day, debating and discussing things at one location, then the next; the 50- and 60-somethings join them after work for beer and cigarettes. What's most curious is how tightly they sit together, and how animated their conversations appear, as if life or death depends upon them discussing whatever it is that they have to share.

As someone passes by, they pause between secrets to which no one else is privy. Especially women. Rarely do they include a woman in their company. (Naturally, the conversation must also stop in order for them to give a thorough once-over to any woman walking past.) Unless it's a bachelor party, it is much more common for me to see groups of women engage in power catch-ups over cocktails back home than to witness groups of men deep in conversation in the U.S.

One day, after finding six pairs of thickly bespectacled eyes gazing back at mine from Massimo's seats in front of the post office in Bagnoregio, I mused to Tony, "What it is that these men talk about all the time?"

Without hesitation, he quipped, "Many important things: shoes, and ships, and sealing-wax. Of cabbages—and kings—and why the sea is boiling hot, and whether pigs have wings." It was so apt that I thought he divined these words spontaneously; he drolly reminded me that this is a quote from Lewis Carroll's "The Walrus and the Carpenter."

We've tapped into that phrase—"cabbages and kings"—every time since that we've encountered these enrapt men, as we did during yesterday's trip to Lago di Bolsena and the hill towns of Castiglione in Teverina, San Sebastiano, Civitella d'Agliano, and Lubriano. Helen, Tony, Bernardo, and I drove through the narrowest of alleys to see these picturesque *paese* which, while full of character, do not have the majestic presence of Civita. Just when I think I have learned to appreciate this place, I travel somewhere else and see even more how well preserved and special it is on my return.

Yet, over lunch with Tony and Helen at Antonio's *bruschetteria* today, I realized that the one place I don't see all-male gatherings is Civita. We discussed yesterday's adventure with longing: Luca's *giardino*, views of the Tiber River Valley, seeing the men in their chairs from town to town, and the outstanding *coregone* fish that we ate in Lago di Bolsena: tender white meat caught mere feet away, the only place they live.

Like a table of Italian men, our own conversation suddenly took an animated turn as I voiced a desire that has been growing for weeks: to start a NIAUSI food institute, perhaps in partnership with Slow Food. Though I wasn't around to participate in her famous didactic dinners, food preparation and shared meals were important teaching tools for Astra. Likewise, those who visit return home revering their cooking lessons with Tony.

I thought back to the "Friends & Fellows" meal that I convened in July as the part of my project; all who attended left feeling more connected, inspired, and gifted with a larger slice of the world seen through someone else's eyes.

While design is typically part of a NIAUSI Fellow's experience in Civita, the idea that we could add a layer of instruction in the cultivation and cooking of local food—as well as the social component of gathering around those meals—seems a logical next step to me. Helen suggested that we include a NIAUSI café with the food institute, and the next thing we knew, we both committed to living in Civita each May through October to run it.

Of course, with all this excitement, there are sobering elements, like funding and tempo. Too much change too quickly will kill the magic here; yet, there are strong agrarian roots that could be nurtured to grow something very authentic and fortifying for Civita's culture, economy, and natural environment through urban agriculture and cooking.

Not to build upon these strengths seems a waste. After all, if tourism remains as Civita's only mainstay, there will never be a revival of resident households—and therefore no chance at a rebirth of the gatherings of men outside Peppone's Bar or Antonio's *bruschetteria*, as I'm told once existed.

But perhaps a couple of passionate women—their heads together in animated conversation—can inspire new growth in Civita—first cabbages, then queens and kings.

23 settembre: Go Girl, Seek Happy Nights to Happy Days

In celebration of Helen's last full day in Civita, we set off on our final Bagnoregio adventure: for me, an investigation of religious iconography, for Helen, unique doorways.

Driven by the powerful curiosity of two, this walk was a continuation of last night's after-dinner stroll, which began on Civita's *decumanus maximus* under a nearly full moon. Lamp light and brilliant pools of moonlight transformed our *passagiata* into a secret garden exploration under the watchful eyes of the Madonna. We experienced a similar sense of covert thrill as we discovered each icon today, squealing softly with delight, our hushed voices echoed gently in the alleys—each found edifice was a prize.

We found countless treasures in the quiet alleys that I've longingly passed for weeks: old and new *porte*, inset sculptures in relief, painted tiles, photographs of saints. We learned that some alleys connect at the cliff's edge, offering a breathtaking view of the valley below, while others lead to quiet, cool courtyards draped in vines.

As I snapped a photo of my favorite icon, I relished the irony of people "finding" religion, and the fact that Helen and I were quite determined and successful in doing just that. It also brought to mind when she commented yesterday about how Civita's setting has the effect of a convent or monastery, providing vast space to quietly reflect.

I realize now how lucky I am to have had the opportunity to inwardly expand into that monastic seclusion during my first six weeks. The coveted solitude of those first days provided an opportunity for intense observation and complete immersion, which now allows me to bloom outward and enjoy the fruits of the relationships I've made—with people and with Civita itself.

After a chance meeting with Luca and his faithful companion, Ito, in Piazza Cavour, Helen and I stopped for *cappuccini* at Massimo's Bar. On this visit, I felt compelled to ask if our server was indeed the infamous Massimo, and sure enough, I found my holy grail. I shared greetings from Stephen and Lucy back home, after which Massimo insisted on bringing us something in addition to our *cappuccini*. Knowing that it's unwise to refuse when Italians offer food, we remained to enjoy *spritz* with chips and olives, an offering for which Massimo wouldn't allow us to pay.

Our pilgrimage home led to lunch with my newly arrived friends, Sue and Kirstin, where we enjoyed *bruschette, gnocchi, pollo* and *stracceti* at Emanuela and Raphaele's *osteria*, followed by her gratis tribute of *espresso* and *biscotti*. We kissed and hugged her goodbye, leaving with instructions on where to find heavenly *gelato* during our trip to Orvieto *domani*.

Beginning with Helen's arrival, and compounded by Sue and Kirstin's visit, I have witnessed a sudden and profound sense of cohesive generosity in my life here. It derives partly from my new role as tour guide, partner, and emissary, a position from which I can karmically repay the innumerable kindnesses that I've received during my stay. I've reached that sweet spot of knowing residents for long enough to begin taking my relationships—and working knowledge of Civita and Bagnoregio—a bit farther.

Adventures here do seem to spring to life spontaneously, as if Civita recognizes people who desire to connect and reflect. Over time in this small place, we become more obvious to each other rather than strange; with each chance meeting we become more revealed rather than protected; with every meal and glass of wine we discover something new, even about old friends; and in the company of each other—even in the dark of night—we find courage to seek out new paths in ancient places.

To enter Civita with a sense of openness, to listen to Italian opera, to discuss—and listen to others speak of—history and politics, poetry, and decades-old friendships has helped to intensify the ways in which Helen and I investigated this place and ourselves within it.

I can't say that I'm religious, but these truths do bolster my sense of faith, though I do credit Helen's and my experience as a reflection of what we've brought to the table. As much as we two have been transformed, and will carry that sensation with us when we depart, it's also possible to come here, click photographs, and leave happy but measurably unchanged.

We've been quoting bits of Shakespeare lately, as I'm in the middle of reading an Italian version of "Romeo and Juliet" to improve my language skills. With a similar sense of faith that our friendship—and our relationship with Civita—will continue long after we find each other again in Seattle, I felt my breath catch at the end of last night's walk.

Turning to blow down a kiss as I ascended my balcony, I felt a new dimension of a familiar phrase as Helen called to me, "Goodnight, Gabriela. Parting is such sweet sorrow."

Ten

"Food and wine feed our connections with people, who are ultimately the story of a place."

10 settembre: Chicken and Figs

Understanding idioms—and employing them correctly—is part of language learning that happens in layers over years; for non-native speakers, it takes a lifetime. In Venezia, Iole and I spent the better part of 15 *minuti* trying to understand why Italians say, *"Ti va…"* when they're asking someone if they'd like to do something.

First, we debated which verb was being conjugated: *volere* or *andare*? It's *andare*, we agreed, but why is it conjugated for him/her/it rather than for the familiar "you?" Aha! We realized that the idiom is asking, "Does it go for you?" (*ti* indicates the familiar accusative case) or more loosely, "Could you go for…" That phrase isn't obvious, although it makes sense.

Idioms aside, I've felt confident enough in my language skills to shop in Bagnoregio without ever bringing my dictionary, which was fine until I visited the *macelleria* to buy chicken. When the butcher asked which part I wanted, I was stuck. The word for chicken (*pollo*) was familiar, but I did not know the word for 'breast.' I sputtered for a few seconds, watching his brow knit, then I did as the Italians do: I pantomimed. He tried not to smile as I gestured with enthusiastic open palms in front of my own breasts, stifling a chuckle as he nodded and said, *"Petti."*

Of course. Like *pectoralis*. Italian isn't that difficult…if you use common sense before speaking. I left with pink cheeks, giving him a story to tell his buddies at Massimo's bar that night.

When I learned that Marco's wife, Inga, is not a native Italian speaker, I thought perhaps I had found someone who would understand what it feels like to be a foreigner amongst natives, even

though we're from very different home countries. Plus, after five years of studying German, it's the one foreign language that pops in my head whenever I struggle for Italian words.

Tony and I met Inga, Marco, and their college-aged children, Niko and Nina, for pizza last night in Lubriano. In spite of Tony's praise, we were unsure of the *pizzeria's* credentials: the place was deserted (*naturalamente*, it was only 19:30 *ore*) and the menu featured over 100 pizzas (one with Nutella, another with mayonnaise and ketchup, and one called "Viagra"...) Curiously, rather than awards for their pizza, we noted that the owners displayed rows of trophies for their fishing accomplishments.

Tony is never wrong when it comes to food, of course; when our food arrived, it was *buonissimo*. Digging into my *pizza con funghi,* I considered our layering of languages. Inga doesn't speak English but she speaks fluent German and her Italian is quite good while Tony and Marco are fluent in Italian and English. Drawing on several languages among us, we made it work—even if some sentences were spoken with a mix of two or all three. It comforted me that, like me, Inga asked for proper pronunciation and words she didn't know in Italian, though her vocabulary is much more extensive than mine.

While we discussed our delicious food, Inga also complimented Tony's *prosciutto* and fig pizza, at which Marco, Tony, and Nina cracked up. Inga and I were mystified. At their laughter, she instantly cringed, asking what she said wrong. Marco explained in a mix of German and Italian, but I still didn't understand, other than that she'd made *un sbagliato*—a mistake.

Marco explained calmly in English, "It's a mistake. She wanted to say figs—*fichi*—but the word she used was not figs. It means, how do you say in English...pussy." Thinking back to my many *sbagliati*, I smiled knowingly at Inga, who turned a fig-worthy shade of purple as I assured her that it was not a big deal.

When we re-entered Civita after 22:00 *ore*, buffeted by icy winds on *il ponte,* I was surprised to find six men in their mid-50s hanging banners for Sunday's donkey race in the Piazza S. Donato. As we walked past them, they sang something that loosely translates to, "Good evening, Germans, we don't speak any German here!" Inga laughed before she and her whole family sang back, "Good evening, Italians, we don't speak any Italian here."

Remarkable in the dark of night, the song and response brought me back to consider the questions I posed just yesterday about the legacy of memory in Civita. Marco and his family are known here by the most random of people. For however long they visit each year, they make an effort to form relationships and traditions—and they are teaching their children to do the same. In light of how many German tourists I hear every day, perhaps their "non-native" heritage could actually be a positive layer atop the strong Italian foundation some day.

So, how many "real" Civitonici are there? Each day, I'm discovering that there are more than I think, and that there are many kinds. I waved hello to Inga and her fab foursome as they ate lunch at Antonio's *bruschetteria* this afternoon, feeling a warm wave of delight to acknowledge people I know on the street, as if Civita is my own neighborhood.

Inga's face lit up as she returned my greeting. Yes, I thought—between my chicken and her figs, we definitely understand one another.

24 settembre: The Path to Something Greater

As my experience layered a solitary exploration of Civita with an impromptu partnership with Helen—and a heartfelt reunion with my friends, Kirstin and Sue—I am again preparing for a different stride on Monday.

But first, in honor of Helen's departure, we closed certain loops with today's visit to Orvieto, gazing with awe at frescoes from the *quattocentro* in the city's *duomo*. Only from viewing the Sistine Chapel had I seen such depictions of judgment, resurrection, and demons raining red blows from fiery swords. Naturally, the scale of Orvieto's chapel is significantly smaller, but the detail is what struck me; at first, when my eyes saw the brutal swaths of thin red paint spread atop the perfectly painted forms, I wondered if the frescoes had been vandalized. The very violence of the color and the clean but thin strokes was startling enough convey the power of evil and torment.

Helen and I discussed for several minutes the stark accuracy of Jesus' gray skin tone in another scene, as Mary takes down his wrecked body from the cross, sharing a moment of our own private losses and spontaneously embracing each other in the center of the chapel. The whole day had a bit of that somber feeling; we were delighted to be in Orvieto and certainly to be together, but her imminent departure was ultimately what called us there.

On our way to lunch, she and I fulfilled a common goal: purchasing *passatutti*—Italian strainers that will allow us to make Tony's tomato sauce after we return to Seattle. (We have vowed to christen them together.)

When we entered Trattoria dell'Orso for our meal, we were greeted by Gabriele and Ciro, who spoke of Tony *("magnifico, molto gentile")* and Astra ("genius!") with such affection that I was reminded of their profound influence on not only Civita, but elsewhere and on people all over the world. Of course, these men who greeted us were not architects, but artisans of the table; yet, it was Astra and Tony's sense of design—as well as their generous spirits—that Gabriele and Ciro praised.

Helen and I walked arm-in-arm on our way out of Orvieto, and *due baci* cheek-kissed goodbye at the train station. I dove into the passenger seat as the *l'autobus* behind us honked at me for holding up traffic. On the drive back to Civita, I reflected on the coincidence that brought Helen and I here, and what we've vowed to accomplish together at home and abroad.

At the root of it all, not so strangely, is food. Both University of Washington alumni and NIAUSI Fellows invariably say that one of the most powerful ways they learned about design, place, the world, and themselves was by cooking with Astra and Tony. Not only by reading, sketching or studying but by preparing, cooking, and sharing food and wine did they learn about presentation and design for living.

With much thanks to Tony for sharing his intelligence, his kitchen, and his relationships along the way, I realized that—much like Astra and Tony's students before me have realized—without food, my experience of Civita would be pale. Food and wine are not mere incidental pleasures here; they are a way and a means—in some cases, the only means—of getting to know this place, including the people.

Without sharing food and wine, I would never have bonded with Gaia and Bernardo. Without them, there would have been no tour of Luca's garden. Without sharing food, I would not have become a part of the circle dance in the *piazza* with Maria and Marcella, nor would I have been able to invite Nilde to our table for a drink last night. Without an intentional focus on meals and food in Civita, I would never have been able to kiss and hug Emanuela after lunch with Kirstin and Sue, during which she doted on us like family. Without sharing food and wine at Antonio's *bruschetteria*, I would not have been invited to witness Elena's baptism, a rare moment to welcome the newest descendant of the Civitonici.

And, of course, one of the most profound experiences of Helen's journey (and my own) in Civita was cooking with each other; a sharing of food and wine that will undoubtedly lead us to future adventures. *In somma*, food and wine have helped to connect us with people who are ultimately the history, meaning, and future of Civita. While its stones may withstand time, people are what truly holds the greater meaning of the place.

As I consider how deeply that the power of a meal has taken me into important everyday places, such as restaurants, homes, churches, cellars, tunnels, gardens, and people's private lives, my belief in the importance of food as an educational tool and catalyst for change continues to strengthen.

On Monday afternoon, I'll be on my own again, though I'm eagerly anticipating those last ten days in Civita. Perhaps it's because I won't be really alone. I will continue my discovery of alleys and icons as I wish the ladies *buon giorno* in passing. I will cook meals with Tony as we listen to opera. I will stop for a Campari soda with Massimo to discuss life in Bagnoregio after I shop at the Mancini sisters' *alimentary*. I'll perch on my balcony so that I can hear impressions about Civita from the influx of American tourists below. They will assume that I'm Italian.

In writing this, I hoped to help readers hear, smell, see, taste, touch and feel everything special about this place so that they could visit it with intelligence some day. There may seem to be a lot of food and wine with each lesson, but I've come to see that a meal, large or small, is not only a necessary ingredient to Italian stories, but always leads to something greater.

8 Settembre: The Elements of an Italian Meal

They say that two things are inevitable in life: death and taxes. Upon being awakened by banging hammers and a concrete mixer, I'd like to submit a third: construction.

Padding to the window to find Giorgio, pounding away in his blue shirt and khaki pants at the facade of *la chiesa*, I muttered, "Isn't this supposed to be a dying city?! "

Pointless to attempt more sleep, I found consolation in the peach-colored clouds tinted by the rising sun. They were so striking that I wandered in my pajamas toward Mary of the Incarcerated to watch the clouds and fog pass each other in the valley.

Later, I realized that an early start didn't translate to a more productive day as I made lunch, leisurely heating up anchovy pasta sauce with *orrechiette*, baptizing sliced cucumber with white wine vinegar and salt, and wrapping quartered figs with *prosciutto*—the quintessential summer Italian meal. Flavorful and elemental.

Such fundamentals remained with me all afternoon, as I continued to ask myself why life is so different here. Everything around me—the architecture, the pace, the food—spoke the same words: penetrating simplicity.

From outside Il Nuovo, one sees tufa stone, tile, wood and metal; other than stucco walls, the interior palette is nearly identical. From entry and kitchen to bed and bath, the exposed stone and wood bring the house together in rustic fitness while the stucco skin reveals a tapestry of natural imperfections, blanketed in white.

Above all, the composition and materials are simple. Honest. Real. The effect of this is comparable to sensing each unique ingredient—and its ability to evoke the flavors of its counterparts—in Italian cooking.

Consider the dinner that Tony and I prepared last night: we chopped and sautéed onion in butter, added *risotto* and *brodo*, then baked it for 20 minutes. While the pilaf cooked, we dredged little octopi called *moscardini* in flour and fried them until their tiny suckered tendrils curled up into dark, crunchy spirals. The *moscardini* were finished as the rice emerged from the oven; we layered rice at the bottom of a dish, placed the fried octopi on top and garnished with lemon wedges. Onion, butter, rice, broth, olive oil, *moscardini*, flour. Simple.

Just as dark wood and the underside of roof tiles make stucco appear more clean and white, the lemon enhanced the rice and the oil brought out the salty sea flavor in the *moscardini*.

The more intently I gazed through this lens of simplicity, the more I found it throughout Civita. Clothes dry on the line. Fresh eggs require no refrigeration. Gratis *espresso* and anise *biscotto* from Emanuela, who spotted me sitting next to the Osteria al Forno d'Agnese writing notes and taking the sun for the few minutes it shined.

She offered coffee yesterday, which I didn't take, but I sense that it's wise to say yes when someone—especially Emanuela—insists twice. On such a blustery day, the *osteria's* patio was empty at 14:30 *ore*; she and her crew were already cleaning up before the major thrust of the storm hit.

Bustling from table to table, her apron flying about her trim frame, Emanuela had time to show me a photo of her son, ask about my work, direct the staff, tease me for thinking she said 'Toscana' when she said 'Tuscania' (two very different places), and then lavish this treat on me. The wind rushed about us, blowing the shamrock green napkins about as I tried to pick up her words, as she speaks *molto velocemente*.

I'm learning that, in a country divided by dialects, culture, north, south, politics, and the mafia, food never fails to unify—it is a tender way to care for others, especially in an age when people are conditioned to look out for themselves. When so many things can easily divide passionate people, it's even more important to be generous with that which connects us, like the simple components of an Italian meal.

The Rest is Silence

Silence is a morning that begins with fog—prisoner clouds are born on the ground and sentenced to hover around Civita all day, swirling and churning, but never dismissed.

Silence is air fully pregnant with humidity, the kind that blends with perspiration to create something salty, dewy and delicious at the nape of one's neck, tempting someone to lick it.

Silence is block after block of wooden doors closed tight, locked by invisible people who are neither there, nor wish you to be.

Silence is a perching gargoyle awaiting the approach of strangers, hearing the scuff and shuffle of their unsuspecting feet, the carefree exclamations of *"Che bella!"* and the electronic click of cameras, a thunderous herd of children pushing, crying, teasing, laughing—until they enter the courtyard and freeze at the sight of you sitting there, unblinking.

Silence is stones so layered with ancient lichens that their dust has turned into a quilt of off-white stains branded into the tufa, inseparable.

Silence is the thin smell of dry, old leaves gathered in corners, the drifting scent of a cigarette, and the aroma of wet, loamy earth mixed with oven-fired bread baked for tourists who aren't there.

Silence is the slapping film reel sound of a moth's frantic wings on geranium leaves.

Silence is a circumspect man who never reveals his secrets—if he has any—but only plods forward wordlessly, step by step, *piano piano,* to sit on a hard stone bench and stare right back at you.

Silence is the clang of milky lantern glass against a rusted frame in time with the pulse of the breeze.

Silence is unyielding stone benches and steps—no proper backrest, no ergonomic height—which tells how hard life must have been if such hard things were ever restful reprieves.

Silence is the clapping of leaves against each other in the breeze, rushing back and forth like waves breaking rhythmically on the shore.

Silence is hundreds of eyes staring out from the darkness as spiders diligently string their webs in the frames of rotted cellar doors where no human has stepped for years.

Silence is the moment you realize that you're either grateful for interruption when it arrives, or deeply annoyed when you've lost it.

Silence is a question, a sense of upcoming change—the quiet before the storm, the bended knee, the transition of seasons—the anticipation of an offer not yet arrived, one that you're unsure you'll accept.

Until it isn't, silence is.

Eleven

"The answer rests in learning to close our mouths and open our hearts, minds, and senses."

27 Settembre: Appropriately Revealed

Humbling and heartwarming is how I best describe hearing stories from a man who has come to know Civita through his 27 years of explorations.

Brothers Ron and Jerry Satterlee arrived this evening to share stories over a rice pilaf with succulent sautéed calamari in the center. I asked them to sing for their supper, delighted by their claustrophobia-inducing tales of larger-than-life snakes—and the time when Alessandra's grandmother, Vittoria, interrupted the mass to demand why the new priest couldn't wait to begin until everyone [read: she] was in attendance. Her lesson has become tradition, as no mass that I've attended has ever begun on time.

Naturalamente, many people have been involved with Civita and NIAUSI long before me, but hearing Jerry's stories in person took me to a yet unknown layer of knowledge and memory that exists about Civita—a layer in which many of the characters are already deceased.

In fact, tonight was the first night that I heard Vittoria or Domenica's names (Domenica, the great grandmother of Elena, who was just baptized.) The concept of time plays games with me again: just when I believe that I understand a part of the sequence, someone adds new ingredients.

Hearing these new names from Jerry, and learning that his own daughter was baptized here (Vittoria is her godmother) hearkens me back to a thought I had yesterday as I wrote about Elena and Alberto: I've witnessed their baptisms, and they will be alive to experience Civita long after I'm gone. In terms of reference points, we are all mere blips in a very long series of moments.

What seems most *proprio* is allowing things to be appropriately revealed over the right periods of time. One person's lifetime—or even the life spans of a person's children and grandchildren—are nothing in comparison with the span of Civita.

These revelations can be found in stories from people like Jerry, who dared to crawl through a long passage no wider than himself to discover a tiled Etruscan room somewhere in the depths of Civita. He found many things during his journeys over the years that will always remain with him, a triumph of sorts over time.

The trick in building upon moments and memories is to begin with a solid foundation. Knowing who you are and why you're present is the bedrock of a life journey. For Jerry, the framework of his Civita memories include those early investigations when he found things like caves, as well as himself.

How can one create a true sense of self without a deep understanding of one's own motivations, weaknesses and strengths? When something is strong and meaningful by nature—Jerry's memories and what he learned from then, or even the bedrock of Civita herself—it forms a solid footing on which he can build a greater understanding of life over time.

I realized tonight that it's possible to be a part of Civita even if I'm never a Civitonicia myself. I can become involved in people's lives and events, see a lifetime of progression in a home's *restauro* and a baptism. My own limited perspective—that of an outsider—can also be what strengthens my observations, allowing me to consider this place from many points and through many lenses. Civita can reveal to me a unique picture that someone "too native" might not see.

As with anything—buildings, lifetimes, relationships—success only comes from a combination of the right time to build, demolish, and restore. Bringing a sensitivity and modesty about what materials to employ, what to leave hidden and at rest, and what to reveal—well, that's an elusive art.

Over a month and a half into my investigation of Civita's layers, I can confirm that only a place with such good bones could continue to reveal such appropriate lessons over time.

28 settembre: Civita stands

While rules are highly subject to interpretation and selective adherence in Italian culture, Americans prefer the illusions of certainty: handbooks, manuals, and time tables. We like to research our vacations with guides, on-line ratings, and advice from friends on where to go and what to see, planning each moment months in advance of stepping outside our homes.

Watching this week's influx of American tourists invade Civita has reminded me of how removed I've been until now. My first six weeks of English blackout were an important gift: I spoke primarily Italian and was able to detach from life in Seattle in order to focus on my work here. Even listening to the European tourists was a learning experience, since most visitors spoke Italian, German, or French.

On Sunday night, Gaia exclaimed with disappointment, "What happened to your Italian?! Why are you speaking English?" It became apparent that I had unwittingly emerged from the purity of my Italian immersion. Could it be my exposure to American tourists?

Contrasted with the Italian chatter that I've heard since *agosto*, the American commentary grates; when someone uses the word, "cute," to describe Civita, I cringe. (Italians use much richer language: *bello, tranquillo, meraviglioso, paradiso…*)

As a self-appointed U.S. ambassador, I dislike seeing how many Americans come here without preparing to speak even simple requests in Italian. They rarely venture further than their travel guides, which seem to provide an invisible bubble of assured, well-managed fun. When things go awry, they appear virtually paralyzed without instruction from an authoritative source—very different from most Europeans who prefer blurry lines and will explore anything anywhere (including my hanging laundry.)

As I considered these behaviors, I thought back to Tony's favorite line, "Nature *IS*," which absolutely fits Civita. Nature is neither good nor evil; it just IS. In the same light, Civita just *IS*; it stands. Period.

The finality of that statement hints at the Civita's immovability which is not so much defiant as it is strong or persistent. Civita has withstood earthquakes, floods, landslides, wars, time, and extreme weather. If it can manage to survive or respond to these awesome forces, it should be a signal that we may need to bend to this experience rather than expect Civita to submit to our control.

Civita gently (or, perhaps not so gently) dares to see if we'll resist or fail her tests. She deters us with the topography of the initial climb, where we find ourselves sweaty and gasping for air. She displays seemingly locked doors and private gardens—the facade of a "cute ghost town," as one tourist remarked. She waits to see if we'll get frustrated and leave, or if we'll bend to the experience to discover something only perceptible by those with intuitive perspectives.

Unable to completely tune out their endless commentary, I'm tempted to correct statements like, "Guess we'll turn around; there's nothing here," or, "That *piazza* would be nicer if they'd fix it up, but I guess nobody lives here anymore. Wanna get a bottle of olive oil before we leave?" Then, I realize that these people aren't so terrible; they just aren't in the same frame of mind.

At one limited extreme, there are tourists who don't dare to venture down the bend past my writing rock. Then there is Jerry's courage in crawling through a tunnel to discover a 2,500-year-old Etruscan oubliette where Vittoria's husband, Luigi, once hid from the Nazis. He seems a rare example of an open, yet self-guided person. When others bring so little sense of adventure—or self-reliance—with them, no wonder they leave Civita somewhat perplexed or disappointed.

Admittedly, living here is what really changes one's experience, and Civita only erects illusory roadblocks. The average tourist is just that because she cannot fathom hauling her cookies all the way uphill to stay longer than an afternoon.

Again, Civita stands.

One could confuse bending to Civita's powers—Nature, Love—with weakness or surrender, but it is in bending that we actually discover our own strength. Only by approaching new places with a sense of curiosity and flexibility can one gain access to greater depths that may not initially reveal themselves.

The more rigid we are, the more we insist that people speak our language rather than trying to learn theirs. The more that we desire familiar products from back home, and the more we hesitate from exploring unmarked paths, the farther removed we become from the possibility of exploring the world—and each other. We might be able to say that we've been somewhere physically, but we can never really know places, people, our even ourselves very well.

When I count how many of Civita's seemingly closed doors have opened for me, how many locked gardens into which I've found entry, and how many fests that I've witnessed in our *piazza*, the more sure I am that the answer rests in learning to close our mouths and open our hearts, minds, and senses. This takes time, patience, and the humility—and strength—to bend to the experience.

Civita stands, indeed. Of course, it takes time to know that.

One Ray the More, One Shade the Less

Do I have enough of your trust that you'll allow me to rouse you from your warm covers before sunrise on a chilly morning? Have we been together long enough for you to know that you won't be disappointed in what you'll find?

That's what Civita seemed to ask me this morning as my right eye opened, followed by my left, just before the 7:00 *ore* bells began to ring. I've been thinking for weeks about waking early to discover the sunrise, but the moment did not feel opportune until today; every experience has its right time.

From bed, I could see the world barely clinging to nighttime—the sky, the rooftops, the alleys, the tufa—all shrouded in bruised shades of purple, the same color as the early morning hollows underneath my eyes. Compelled, I tossed back the comforter and pulled on my glasses, jeans, and a sweatshirt, circling my black pashmina around my neck and mouth, like a bedouin wrapped against the desert.

The sky's tint bled from aubergine to Campari red on the skyline, then a bright *arancia* in time for me to reach the bend at the end of the street next to the forbidden garden. As soon as the sun pulsed its sulphuric scald over the edge of the mountain range, the shades of purple fell like heavy velvet to reveal a gossamer red drape that instantly warmed my naked toes.

Like arriving just as a play begins, I wondered if I might have missed an important prologue when I sat down on the stone step with quiet attention.

Sunrise in Civita... a giant flower with a white-hot corona so scalding that its after-image remained burned in my retinas even minutes after looking away. As my vision cleared, I noticed a light haze hanging in the valley, the heavy, cold air pulling vapor down to the earth, as if it could hide there from the sun's laser light. Down in the mist, roosters crowed back and forth, their calls punctuated by a donkey's raspy *hee-haw*, one and then the other.

As the tufa burned an even brighter red—a wall of warm coals to my left—the sun's light revealed thick interweaving snail-trails: a golden, glittery network of iridescent threads where I've only ever seen soft, dull rock.

Like the progressive colors in a lava lamp, the light turned from crimson to green, reflecting the chlorophyll in all of the plants that surrounded me. A colony of mossy spots on the wall at my right were still damp with dew and soft like my seaweed green chenille pillows back home. As my fingers explored those cool, downy mounds, I heard a babbling brook through a nearby grate: the sweet gurgling sounds of gray water running through secret passages all the way down to Viterbo.

Brighter and brighter, shifting from emerald green to a warm, juicy flood of Fanta orange, the sunlight sought out and destroyed dark corners one by one. I looked up from the retreating shadows to find a half-full moon directly overhead, bold in its reflection as the sun in its projection.

Selene refused to cede the sky. I've never witnessed the moon stand so firm against a coming dawn.

A kennel of dogs yapped madly for their breakfast down in the valley as I took in the flawless crystal-blue panorama of sky, which foretold of *un buonissimo giorno d'inverno* ahead. The mists began to rise, giving the chalky *calanchi* mountains a white canvas backdrop while the lower hills grew dimmer beneath them from the rising gray steam.

Dead leaves played follow-the-leader in a small cyclone at my feet as I snuggled deeper into my pashmina, my fingertips turning icy numb. It was only then that I could smell the dryness in the air—that crisp, autumn odor laced with a hint of smokiness that pries humidity from us as we breathe. Summer is truly over.

In the wind's whip of the dry reed grass to brush my arm, there was suddenly full daylight around me, thrusting me from a sultry sonnambulist's journey into the expected daytime enchantment of Civita. The snail trails had disappeared, and now I saw the same sunshine on the rocks that everyone sees—that yolky yellow Lazio light that inspires the lamps to seethe golden at night.

As if to conclude the program, the gentle thunder of a jet roared above me on its way to Rome, where I'll find myself next week, but the con trail was lost in the blue.

Twelve

"I already know that the value of every day spent in civita will increase a hundredfold for each one that I'm away."

14 settembre: The Once and Future Fellow

Typically, on days that I don't walk to Bagnoregio for groceries (also known as my cardio workout), I practice yoga on the stone floor of Il Nuovo. In lieu of today's practice, I showed up at Tony's in the late morning to assist him in preparing a meal for four Americans from Lynchburg, Virginia, two of whom are visiting homeowners.

As I have many times during the past week, I once again challenged myself to define Civitonici. This couple has owned a home in Civita for 15 years, which they visit a couple of times each year. While they're away, they lend their home to friends or rent it out, as do most Italians who own homes here. What is different, of course, is that these are Americans.

Though American, they are indeed connected with Civita, with Astra and Tony, and with the other Civitonici, including the Rocchi family, ("We need to get us some of that Rocchi *rossi*! Can you get Sandro on the phone and have him deliver it tonight?" Frank called to Tony as soon as they entered.) Yes, they own a home in Civita, but they are in every way—language, culture, accent, lifestyle—not the same as other part-time I've met. Throughout lunch I asked myself: could they ever be called Civitonici?

Today also marks the brief return of Ilaria and Bernardo, here for two days from Rome as Ilaria, a landscape architect, consults with Luca at his *giardino*. I felt thrilled to receive her email asking to dine together, as if we were old friends. I realized that the reason it felt so good was that this is exactly what Civitonici do when they discover that they've both dropped into town at the same time.

After nearly five hours of preparation, eating, and clean-up, our Lynchburgers' lunch wiped out most of my afternoon writing time. The gentle buzz from Tony's supply of Rocchi wine didn't help, either. I stepped out to *fare una passagiata* to clear my head, circling *vicino* Josè's empty house. Then I stood by the high wall near the Marchesa's *palazzo* to take a little sun. Ever in search of a comfortable seat amongst all this stone, I walked back through Via Mercatello with a nod to Maria, who attempted to wave me and a few tourists into her *giardino* for a Euro.

I looked with new eyes upon the gate that Fabrizio and I scaled, continued out Civita's back road where I found a fantastic outcropping upon which to sit, write, and reflect.

There hadn't been formal introductions when the Lynchburgers arrived, and I noticed that they didn't speak to me at first, which initially had me feeling slighted; later, I learned that they weren't sure if I spoke any English, since I had greeted them in Italian. Similarly, when I answered Tony's phone during lunch with, *"Pronto, "* a woman named Helen, who called to announce her arrival in Lo Studio, assumed that I was Italian, and stuttered a request to speak in English.

Enjoying the breeze from atop my sunny stone, I had a proud, private chuckle: how great does it feel to have people assume first that I am Italian—and have the Italians so quickly welcome me into their lives? What could be more lovely than what I have been learning of secrets behind many of the seemingly closed doors and garden gates here?

As I scribbled several lines, I wasn't at all surprised to watch several couples walk down near me, snap a few photos of the valley, and turn around, missing the discovery of Mary of the Incarcerated and the tunnel that runs underneath the town.

That's when I began to think about my own presence in Civita over time. What role will I play here? Will I be missed in my absence and greeted warmly when I return? How will I leave my own mark?

I began to envision dinners that I would host in the courtyard outside Il Nuovo, or coffee dates with Josè, Maria, Marcella, Gaia, and Bernardo. I pictured long-awaited hugs and wine-fueled conversations in Italian, Tony's opera playing in the background. I started thinking about other pieces I could add to the richness of Civita that involve food and storytelling...

I reflected on Frank's pleasure at hearing Sandro Tractor Man say "Good morning," in English for the first time ever. We all have an effect on each other, a layering of influence over time. That felt like an echo or reflection of my primary goal in this fellowship, which was to begin an experiential dialogue between Civita and people throughout the world—to bring faraway experiences closer together through a personal exploration.

For me, that desire grows ever stronger. When I bring readers along on my daily journeys, I hope to open a door to experiences—sensory or otherwise—far richer than buying a bottle of *limoncello* or a bag of pasta before turning to leave...and missing all of the good stuff.

When I return each year, I hope to see evidence of a personal legacy come to fruition: as I sun myself on what is now my favorite rock, more and more people will pass by, inspired to find Mary and the tunnel below for themselves.

Perhaps 15 years hence, people might begin to consider me an honorary Civitonicia.

2 Ottobre: Value and Worth

When emailing my friend Brad, I used the salutation, '*caro*,' which simply means 'dear' in Italian. He quipped, "*Caro* in Spanish = expensive!" to which I added that *caro* also means expensive in Italian, but either way—relationships or money—the word describes things of value.

Things of value quickly became a prime subject, as I discovered yesterday my debit card was canceled due to fraud. Unfortunately, this also cut off my access to cash. Thankfully, Tony came to my rescue, as I've been unable to get help from Bank of America or Visa. Along the way, we've had many conversations about banking systems, exchange rates, hidden fees, and bureaucracy.

With this in mind, I pondered the ideas of value and worth. What creates something of value in the first place? Something can be deemed valuable if people desire it. Currency notes or gold aren't inherently worth anything, they're just paper scraps and so-called precious metals; it's our prizing of those items that transforms them into valuables.

Naturally, the concept of value can change over time—something that I note whenever I withdraw cash to find that it takes increasingly more U.S. dollars to create one Euro.

The worth of anything and everything can change on a whim: relationships wither, the value of stocks or homes fluctuates wildly, and even our self-worth changes over a lifetime. Some value living in cosmopolitan cities like New York or Paris; to others, the physical challenge of lugging groceries uphill does not outweigh the ultimate value of living in Civita.

When it comes to such places, what allows them to remain desirable? Perhaps after desire comes time. By this, I mean the influences of time, which creates a unique, irreplaceable patina that others find valuable.

As a species, we like old things; they comfort us with a sense of weight and gravitas, as if proximity to something time-honored somehow increases our own longevity. Buildings become legacy: places that we hand down to the next generation, proof that we were here and a safeguard of our family's future, an extension of our own lives. We value time-tested buildings and cities with proven staying power, including ones that call us to rebuild them after they've been demolished by war and disaster.

Caché, too, establishes value. We value things that are unique, rare, and impossible to duplicate. We like things with character because we believe they indicate—or enhance—our own. But we also value things that are authentic, which is often synonymous with age.

These elements come together in Civita. Tourists from across the world are equally delighted by what they find: the ancient stone gate, the *chiesa*, the *decumanus maximus* lined with terracotta flower pots, small winding alleys, tufa stone buildings, post-and-lintel doorways, secret caves with centuries-old olive presses, lush *giardini*, wooden doors, and wood-framed windows—even Tony's gate, which was selected for its appropriateness but is not nearly as ancient as it appears.

There is thoughtful consistency within the materiality throughout Civita, traditions that are still followed today, and people are willing to pay to restore and retain homes in this most unlikely of locations because of the perceived value of living in a unique and well-designed place that symbolizes a life of delight.

Perhaps it's as simple as: *desire + uniqueness + time = value.*

In a nod to how my relationships might change in my absence from Seattle, my friend Jay quoted François de la Rochefoucauld before I left: "Absence diminishes commonplace passions and increases great ones, as the wind extinguishes candles and kindles fire." When I consider what Civita meant to me before I arrived, what it means to me now, and what it will mean in the days after I leave, I must also acknowledge absence or loss as another element in the value equation.

With my return imminent, I am on the verge of discovering the true value of the relationships I left behind in Seattle. I'm also measuring my valuation of Civita from what I've learned during the past seven weeks. Somehow, I already know that the value of every day spent here will increase a hundredfold for each one that I'm away.

Of course, the kindled passion that will increase between this visit and the next will make the arduous climb well worth it.

8 Ottobre: Swan Song

For my entire career, and the changes I made through college and design school, I've struggled with the dichotomy of having jobs that paid well but did not feed me creatively, or suffering for my craft. Until I came to Civita, the two worlds never had the opportunity to meet.

Though it wasn't in my plan, I began my career working for a real estate development firm out of college. Their young VP liked the fact that I was a writer and editor for *The Arizona Daily Wildcat;* I remember him saying that he hired me because, "If you are a good writer, you can do anything."

I thought of Jordan—and Sigmund Eisner, my beloved Chaucer professor—as I entered the church of S. Cecilia in Rome's Trastevere neighborhood today, which is located on the site of the house in which she lived in the third century AD. As I neared a sculpture of her ruined form, two words from an undergraduate term paper on Chaucer's "Second Nun's Tale," which captures the story of S. Cecilia, sounded in my mind: sassy super-heroine.

Legend has it that, when S. Cecilia's body was disinterred in 1599, it was completely intact. That included the slash wounds on her neck, which didn't kill her instantly but from which she bled to death after three days. The patron saint of music, S. Cecilia reportedly sang hymns even after she was attacked with axes by Emperor Severus' men—first, they attempted to suffocate her in her bathhouse, then they tried to cut off her head—but her devotion to a greater idea allowed her to persist in spite of such brutality.

When I contrast who I was in college when she and I first met—what I believed in, my lack of life experience, how separately I held my true self—with the woman I am now, I can see no more fitting closure to this fellowship journey than at S. Cecilia's feet.

She and I together began a path that was based on my love of stories that rang true. Like the bible or ancient mythology, even if the "Canterbury Tales" speak only in metaphor, a person standing against all odds in order to say what she believes is true is something that we all hope we're capable of accomplishing.

It is with a similar sense of faith that my life has converged with S. Cecilia once again, only this time I feel more prepared for our meeting. With the NIAUSI fellowship, I've been able to make flesh what was once a ghost of a dream: writing a book that was real and true.

I've scoured Rome for the past few days looking for a sign, and she is the one I chose. Looking on the most elegant marble sculpture of a woman in swooned repose, a deep gash on her neck as proof of her devotion to what was real and true in her life, I thought to myself: *This is not an ending, but a beginning.*

It's fitting that the final site I visited was dedicated to a woman who spoke her mind to the last, even after the guards attempted to violently silence her. There are things in life that we're all afraid to say; sometimes we get punished for saying them. Yet, the price of not saying how we feel— what is real, what is true—is deeper, not just for the person speaking the words, but for those who might have benefitted from hearing them. Rather than an upfront cost of being real and true, the price of leaving things unsaid seems to double and triple over every year.

Like any continuing saga, the best knowledge rests in the fact that I'll pick up this story when I return to Seattle. This fellowship journey is one chapter—a grand chapter and a marvelous adventure, to be sure—but what I ultimately take from it is only the beginning.

Though my life story has many yet-unwritten parts, this experience has taught me to have faith that they'll happen as they're meant to, in their own time, *piano piano.* That, and I'll never lose faith in the importance of sharing stories and tables...and in my own voice that I know can sing, in spite of adversity.

Thirteen

"Home is a verb."

5 Ottobre: Citizen of the World

It's strangely fitting—*proprio*, one might say—that it's pouring buckets during my last full day in Civita. No need to venture out exploring; this initial expedition is complete.

Beginning yesterday at 15:00 *ore*, thunderheads blackened the sky to a shade so dark that the street lamps turned on, an eerie mid-day warning. From my kitchen window I watched Giorgio, the construction foreman, run this way and that across the scaffolding, holding a feeble tarp over himself while he secured equipment against the howling wind and rain.

The weather kept the construction crew away this morning, much like the tourists and Emanuela, who did not come up from Bagnoregio to open her *osteria* for lunch, much to my disappointment. I was hoping to say a proper goodbye, which I won't be able to do tomorrow, since Tony and I are leaving in the morning for the train station.

In today's notes, I moved toward the conclusion of my experience here, once again contemplating the concept of home. Despite strong desires, perhaps it's actually a gift not to be "from Civita," or even to live here full-time.

Remembering the lesson of an essay that I posted just before leaving Seattle, it's the blend of bitter with sweet that gives a richer and more pleasurable experience than one finds in one or the other. Perhaps the bitter side of knowing that this experience was temporary is what made each day in Civita *molto dolce*. Knowing that life is not like this everywhere is what evokes that deeply protective reverence from those who see its delicate existence as both rare and containing much potential.

When it comes to the concept of home, perhaps the point is not to select a single place of origin, but to hold the best parts of all my beloved cities—Civita, Verona, Venezia, Seattle, San Francisco, Montreal, Paris, NYC—together in the home of my heart.

Being a citizen of the world is not about having a list, but building a portfolio of experiences. It's not about ticking off each city as I visit there, but about building a shared history: a network of meaningful encounters and relationships criss-crossing the globe.

For me, travel is not only about discovery, but ambassadorship. With each journey, I appreciate more what we share as human beings underneath our various customs than about how foreign those customs seem. Feeling understood by people with whom I barely share a common tongue gives me more hope in humanity than anything else.

Earth-shattering revelations and instant relationships do not form overnight or every night. We want everything quickly or we become easily discouraged. Amongst many lessons, Civita has taught me that there is a time and a place for everything, including new places and new friendships, which require space and time to develop at their own speed, in their own time, one by one.

Tomorrow, *io vado a Roma* where I'll rendezvous with José on Thursday, and *la famiglia* Rossi Doria on Wednesday. It's one step toward feeling like a citizen of the world when I can walk into an ancient city and find friends who live there.

At the end of this journey, I am thankful for a changed view of the world, and an enriched perception of myself. Living in Civita has heightened my ability to observe so many important small parts of life with sensitivity and intention, a more powerful lens with which to consider who I am, what I know—what I don't—and what happens next.

Over the past two months, this place has also tempered a momentous patience in me—and an intensified desire to continue my exploration of places at home and abroad.

After all, as a citizen of the world, that's my duty. And my privilege.

7 Ottobre: I'm lost

Nothing confirms that I'm out of my home country like being asked to produce my *documenti* upon request by uniformed *polizia in treno*. While the officer and her partner were clearly in pursuit of someone, it was certainly not me, if the speed at which she reviewed and returned my passport—with a smile, no less—was any indication.

One of the three men from my compartment avoided inquiry by continuing past us when he returned from the restroom to find the officers checking his companions' passports. My intuition trembled, as I wondered if they were looking for him.

In truth, the three of them made me uncomfortable with their stares from the moment I entered the compartment, as did their false cheerfulness to the officers as their passports were called in. It was impossible to tell where they were from based on looks—short, squat, and dark—or their language, which I couldn't identify. The male officer asked if they understood Italian; when they shook their heads, *"Italiano? No,"* he made a disgusted sound and said, *"Non capite niente:"* you don't understand anything.

After the officers returned their passports and moved to the next car, the third man returned to his friends, who laughed about his elusion of the police. Remembering that they had an audience despite the disinterest I feigned, the thinnest of them hailed my attention to inquire, *"Roma?"*

I answered, *"Sì."*

"Italiana?" he asked. I said no. He laughed and said something to his friends, at which one of them looked me over, trying to figure me out, as much as I wondered about them. Suddenly, each of their cellphones rang one by one; my stomach flip-flopped, wondering with whom I was traveling.

For the rest of the trip, it was impossible to feel at ease with the cacophony of their laughter and the increasing volume of their voices in such a small space. I couldn't hide my revulsion at watching the man across from me plug his left nostril and blow mucus out of the right nostril into the window curtain. Irony had me recalling the sunny comment I made about how the little differences need not divide us as humans.

At that moment, I was not only mentally pleading for division, but a sneeze guard.

While increasingly more pleasant than my train ride there, I've spent much of my time in Rome lost. I've even felt lost in the student flat I'm renting, whose rooms house 11 equally uncomfortable single beds.

Walking to dinner at Gaia and Bernardo's home last night, I grossly overshot my mark, instead wandering all the way to S. Giovanni dei Fiorentini on the Tiber River. After asking directions— twice—I retraced my steps and realized that the scale of my map and my mental scale were not in sync. On the map, their house seemed far from my *appartamento* in Campo de'Fiori, but it was actually a mere seven minutes away on Via Giulia, just down the street from Palazzo Farnese.

This morning I was likewise turned around while in search of DuDu, a costume jewelry shop *vicino* Piazza Navona. It took over 30 *minuti* of retracing my steps to realize that, while I had a better sense of scale today, my mental map was turned upside down.

The epiphany occurred as I rested on a marble bench near Fontana del Nettuno after I re-entered Piazza Navona for the third time, frustrated that I couldn't map my position. I took a breath and

thought back to Cafe Sant' Eustachio, which seemed to be in the wrong place when I passed by minutes earlier. I then had to ask: despite what I believed to be true, what if my perception was exactly 180 degrees opposite?

My *aha!* came quickly: since I began my trek by getting lost in a desperate search for *la prima colazione* (breakfast), I had entered Piazza Navona from the opposite end that I intended to enter. After establishing that main data point incorrectly—which side of the *piazza* was "up"—every move I had made since then was incorrect.

Once my vision cleared, I immediately found DuDu in its promised place.

Piano, piano, I corroborated my way from one street to the next, arriving as intended on a string of pearls: the Pantheon, the Fontana di Trevi, and the *ristorante* marked on my map, Vini e Cucina di Nana. It wasn't open yet, so I distracted myself by window-shopping, wherein I quickly fell in love with a shimmering bracelet. The clerk had to buzz me inside the shop, which should have been a clue as to its price, and I was disappointed to discover that the bracelet cost over 1,500 Euro. My second choice, a pair of filigreed earrings, was within range, so I declared, "*Vorrei comprare!*"

While the woman wrapped up my jewelry, we talked about Civita and my trip, which was nearly at an end. She was impressed with how well I spoke Italian after a short immersion (*"Bravissima!"*) to which, I said that I was sad (*triste*) to leave.

As she handed me the gold bag, she advised me not to think that way. *In italiano* she said, "What an adventure! What a time! And now you are in Rome where it's warm and beautiful. Every time you wear these earrings you will think of this trip. Besides, you will return to Italy, no?"

Her sentiments remained with me as I walked into the restaurant, selected *un tavolo al fuori,* and ordered without stumbling over my words. Yes, I was in a beautiful city to which I would certainly return. And yes, I had a marvelous adventure and learned to speak Italian. Why lose myself in a sense of somber longing—an old habit that I thought I kicked—when I could appreciate what was around me and all of the good times leading up to it?

It's funny how a person can continue to get lost in a familiar map, retracing her steps over and over, until a stranger points out that she's headed in the opposite direction.

15 Ottobre : Heart is where the Home Is

While re-acclimating to Pacific Daylight Time, I spent the past four days in Northern California for a grantee retreat supporting my collaboration in a program called *Invoking the Pause.* Our funder, Maggie, drew her grantees together so that we could meet each other, and so that she and her staff could know us personally.

Though we didn't know what to expect, it was no surprise that the experience was emotionally turbo-charged. Our first meeting began with each of us taking turns sharing information around a double circle of 30 people, answering questions such as where we were from and where we called home.

Libby, the first to speak, began to cry as she talked about her home in Pennsylvania, unwittingly establishing a safe and open tone for the rest of the convocation. Others were moved to tears in their speeches before these then-strangers, including me, feeling my eyes grow wet and my voice tremble upon speaking the word, "home."

I explained that I was returning from two months in a place that made me rethink where I belonged. My body was still on Civita time (which meant that it was 1 am when I spoke), my brain was wired to think and speak *in italiano,* and my body was already shriveling with the lack of touch in every interaction.

"What is home?" I asked aloud, hearing the despair in my voice; "I don't think I know anymore." I talked about Seattle and how much I've loved returning to it for the past nine years—until now. Leaving the warm Lazio light to return to a cold, rainy, dark Seattle felt like moving from heaven to purgatory.

I arrived *nel pomeriggio* last Saturday and left for California on Monday morning, happy to re-emerge in Santa Rosa's 85-degree heat. And now... I was unsure where home was. Was it in Civita where I bloomed as a writer and a person? Or was it in the place I once loved, which now seemed more like a storage locker for an apartment full of things I didn't miss?

Later in our introductory session, a woman named Ann suggested that, as a person who has lived all over the world, "Home is not a noun. Home is a verb."

It was cold again when I arrived in Seattle last night, stepping inside my Queen Anne apartment just before midnight. After experiencing insomnia and dizziness in California, I wasn't sure what I was in for. Yet, within the sense of spinning, my surroundings seemed so familiar as to be pedestrian. As I fell asleep, I heard my words to Iole as she and I walked on the Rialto Bridge arm in arm: "When there are places like Civita and Venezia, what does the rest of it matter?"

The next day, when I complimented the flavor of my cappuccino to the server at Le Pichet on First Avenue, she spoke of an impending trip to Italy. We excitedly traded notes about Verona, Venezia, and Civita—a conversation that made my heart swell. Our exchange reminded me of Italy, where it was possible for strangers to share more than shallow niceness over coffee.

As I mixed the espresso into the pert foam, I thought back to Ann's words, and a later echo of them. Before departing the convocation, each of us made an oath by adding one word to the phrase, "I will..." It was no surprise to hear, "I will home," as a shared promise within our group. As we continued around the circle, I both surprised and scared myself by uttering the words, "I will commit."

Perhaps if home is a concept we carry with us—if we commit to making home into an action, a place in our hearts, a stronger sense of self—then it's possible to be at home no matter where our bodies or our possessions reside.

Like being a citizen of the world, the point is not about finding one place where we belong forever or "losing" something when we leave, but about possessing the emotional intelligence to identify when we're in the right place at an appropriate time—and when it's time to move to the next right place.

If heart is where the home is, then there's no need to lament our departure from one country for the next, no matter how beloved it may be. If we're always home, then the world is a menu of experiences that we can order up as our hunger inspires us—again and again, if we desire, or when appropriate, a new dish altogether.

Epilogue

Writing this finale has been, by far, the most challenging piece. Over the past few weeks, I've started no less than ten drafts, scrapping each of them. Every time I began to write, my tone came through stiff and scholarly—absolutely wrong for the conclusion of this adventure.

Last week when I discussed this struggle with Stephen, he questioned the need for a conclusion at all, since my relationship with Civita is far from over. Though I agreed with his thinking, I still felt a need to revisit my original proposal and each of the topics I had proposed to address.

Sitting at a familiar marble table in Caffe Ladro at the bottom of Queen Anne hill, I remembered back to the beginning of this journey when I spent each weekend in November and December 2009 there working on my proposal. While crafting my submission, I convened a council of advisors to help clarify my questions and goals, hoping to present the most compelling case for why NIAUSI should send me—a writer, not an architect—to live in Civita for two months.

As I reviewed my proposal, I cringed at how naive and simple my questions seemed: *What about Civita allows it to remain compelling and endure? What physical and social systems are relevant to our modern lives? Where do natural and man-made systems interact, and how can we recreate this in Seattle? What ancient design truths are relevant to today's cities? What value is created by the layering of time, and how can that value be described, measured, and captured?*

I realized then that my struggle with writing a conclusion was born from a need to prove that my work—and NIAUSI's investment in me—was ultimately worthy. As I set my proposal booklet aside, I reminded myself that my fellowship experience has been successful in large part because of faith rather than facts, in free-form discovery rather than pre-determined paths.

That's when I knew that these closing thoughts should be about what I learned, rather than a justification of how my work "correctly" answers the questions I posed a year ago.

Reflecting on moments like when Sandro held up his hands and urgently advised, *"Piano, piano!"* as I chugged my *cappuccino*, I've come to appreciate the value of time and the importance of place. I can now see how much my behavior has to do with the environment in which I live—how streets and parks are designed, how transportation systems work, how I obtain my food, and how the demands of modern life encourage me to move faster—but farther away from people, nature, and even from my own thoughts.

In my proposal, I talked about green infrastructure, but what I learned in Civita was how valuable a single garden can be. Gathering my meals from the earth changed my life: I discovered where my food came from, I learned that I only needed a few natural ingredients to prepare a delicious meal, and I witnessed the magnetic gathering and healing power of food. In Italy, food and wine do not merely sustain life, but are themselves reasons to live.

While I assumed that I'd be studying architecture in Civita, I never dreamed that everyday living in a small, remote hilltown would actually be a study of life. Whether I walked into Bagnoregio to shop for groceries, accompanied Tony to church, stopped to enjoy a drink at a cafe, or sat on my rock in the sun, I learned something about myself and my place in the world. Together, the warm tufa buildings, the tolling church bells, the steep climb home, and the narrow streets created a fertile playground for my writing—and my emotional development.

Streets, buildings, and gardens aside, the impact of everything I learned boils down to people. Those who live and work in Civita are its lifeblood—they are what makes Civita special and meaningful. It was true 27 years ago when Jerry Satterlee first visited, and it's true today. Seeing how individuals such as Antonio and Emanuela contribute to a sense of place in a small town has shown me that we all take part in the cities in which we live. It can be difficult to discern a single person's impact in places as large as Seattle or Chicago; yet, large or small, we are each threads in a greater tapestry, adding color and texture with our very presence and the choices we make.

Building upon all of this, the greatest thing that I learned in Civita was how to sharpen my focus to see the interconnectedness of everything around me. In that, I've realized how important it is to pause and appreciate beauty—in the blowing leaves of a street tree or the symmetry of a building, in the sticky juices of a ripe peach or in someone's smile as we pass each other on the street. Knowing what to look for is the first step into a larger world.

As the longest night of the year approaches, I think back to the evening when Iole, Denis, and I sat across from a Biennale poster that read: "Days are short when nights are long / Nights are short when days are long." Each statement is true, and it's all about perspective.

The first chapter of my Civita adventure—a long, glorious day in the sun—may be closed, but I've set a strong foundation atop it that will support a lifetime of stories yet unwritten. I now find myself wishing for a summer dream during this long winter's night: one that begins and ends with a gentle tolling of bells, the warmth of yolky Lazio light, the aroma of bread grilled over a fire, and the affectionate embrace of friends gathered around a table underneath a pergola of grapevines.

In gratitude...

My adventures in Civita cannot end without a large offering of thanks. This book is not only the product of my own hand, but the result of overwhelming generosity—and sweat equity—from friends, colleagues, and family.

Profound thanks to my Council of Advisors, beginning with Bonnie Duncan, who introduced me to NIAUSI and suggested that my work would be competitive for this fellowship. A mother-mentor, and a beautiful writer, she continues to inspire me to new heights simply by believing in me.

To Stephen Antupit and Lucy Sloman, and their family—Henry, Natalie, The Goat, Edna Mode, and Fiona (rip)—whose knowledge and experience of Civita helped me at critical milestones along the way. Thank you for food, friendship, and words like *chillaxification*.

To Lee Copeland, a patient and natural teacher whose kind mentorship encourages my creativity in our daily conversations.

To Martha Droge, whose insightful advice helped me to shape my conceptual proposal. Her intelligence, warmth and humor are blessings in my life.

And to Tom Paladino, whose tough questions helped me to clarify my concept, and whose caretaking kept my Seattle world intact while I was away. Thanks for always challenging me to push the line further—and for checking my mail.

Super-spiffy unicorn thanks to Ellen Milne for her beautiful book design, and the time and thoughtfulness she gave to this volume. Her masterful eye for composition and lust for typography is what unifies and celebrates my experience on the page. Thank you for giving form to my words.

Heartfelt gratitude to Stephen Antupit for his editing skillage and his companionship from the beginning. His insight and emotional intelligence have not only influenced this book, but my life. Here's to accelerated serendipity and Campari soda—with a sweet slice of orange.

Grazie mille to Iole Alessandrini, who opened up the magic of Venezia for me with her friendship, warmth, and bright smile. Together, we will always find circles to dance in, *mia amica*.

My experience in Civita would not have been the same without Helen Kim, whose friendship and camaraderie lit up my days, from scaling locked gates and cooking at Tony's to *cappuccino* at our cafe in Bagnoregio and strolling arm-in-arm through Orvieto. I look forward to future adventures on foreign and domestic shores.

Baci to Jonathan Teng for the most excellent introduction to Civita—and for lugging my groceries on the first shopping trip.

To Jerry Satterlee, whose stories brought to life a part of Civita that I never knew existed. Thanks for inspiring me to keep looking—and for the flowers.

Warm thanks to Nicholas Mathieu, for years of friendship and a sharp eye in the final read before we went to print.

To my family and friends whose unwavering support helped to ground me back home: Angela, for hours of much-needed girl chat; Auntie Ellen, Zip, LuLu, Darrell and Jackson, for love; Tammie, for always reading; CityLab7, for partnership and pauses; Tom, Sue and Kirstin, for their adventurous spirits and keeping a place for me at their table; and Jess and Sugar Bear for being the bestest friends ever.

Without the special people who live and work in Civita, this book would fall flat. My deepest thanks for welcoming me into your homes, your lives, and your tables. To Gaia and Bernardo, Ilaria and Marco, Marcella, Maria, Antonio, Rossana, Ivana, Marco and Inga, Sandro, Emanuela and Raphaele, Father Marco, Alessandra, Giovanni, Ludivico, Laura, and *la bella figura,* Josè. Appreciation to the Rocchi family for the best wine and olive oil I've ever tasted—what you create is magic.

Fond thanks to those who took part in my daily life in Bagnoregio: Anna Ri and Gentilli—the Mancini sisters—who made my shopping experience a delight; Maria Grazia, whose fruits and vegetables nourished me as much as her smile; Carla Vittoria at NovaRea for my copy of *"Romeo e Giulietta"*; and to Massimo, for his hospitality.

For their financial support and belief in my work, I offer heartfelt gratitude to NIAUSI. Civita has changed my life in every way; without this fellowship, there would be no book. Special thanks to Tom Miller for his counsel and friendship; Steve Day, my touchstone along the way; and Nancy Josephson for graciously offering their breathtaking home as the venue for my "Friends and Fellows" collaborative dinner.

Finally, my admiration, affection, and thanks to Tony Costa Heywood. For opera and cooking together, for wine and cognac, for church on Sundays, for *risotto con funghi,* for cabbages and kings, for Julia Child, for lazy vowels, for *fiori di zucca,* and for two months of most excellent conversation and companionship.

And to Nerone, my faithful familiar: meow.

Appendix: Recipes

10 Agosto
Prosciutto e Melone
Slice melon thin and wrap with *prosciutto di Parma.*

Riso con Prosciutto e Verdure
Cook rice on stove top and allow to cool. Add chopped celery, minced parsley, julienned ham and thinly sliced and chopped cucumbers. Toss with a light dressing of chopped green olives, olive oil, white wine vinegar, salt and pepper.

11 Agosto
Insalata Mista
Toss shredded radicchio and lettuce, sliced fennel, sliced tomatoes, sliced hard-boiled eggs, and sliced green olives with a dressing of Italian mayonnaise, oil, spicy mustard and salt.

13 Agosto
Risotto ai Funghi
Sauté fresh, sliced porcini mushrooms with butter and a clove of garlic (discard clove after simmering for a few minutes.) When just about finished, add finely chopped parsley.

Boil chicken stock and water and keep warm on the side. Sauté sliced onion in butter; add rice and allow to cook until the edges of the grain become translucent. Add white wine and stir occasionally. When wine boils off, add the stock water bit by bit to let it absorb. Towards the end, add the sautéed mushrooms and stir together. Top with grated Parmesan cheese.

14 Agosto
Torte di Zucchini con Fiori di Zucca
Thinly slice potatoes, zucchini, scallions, ham and gruyere. Add a little cooking spray to a baking dish. Start with a thin layer of flowers, then alternate potatoes, zucchini, onions, ham and cheese. (Use 2 to 1 zucchinis and potatoes to the ham, cheese and scallions.) Salt the two potato layers.

End with the rest of the flowers spread out on top. Then pour a mixture of 3 eggs and 3 TBSPs of flour over the top of the casserole. Bake it for 40 minutes at 350 F.

19 Agosto
Melanzane al Forno
Slice eggplants to ¼ inch and fry in oil until cooked through. Drain on paper towels. Cut buffalo mozzerella to slices of the same thickness.

On the stovetop, cook down onions and tomatoes in olive oil, then run through a sieve to create pulp. Spray down a baking pan with non-stick spray and alternate slices, eggplant and cheese. Cover modestly in the tomato pulp and then complete another layer.

Cover in grated Parmesan cheese and bake for 25 minutes at 350 F.

3 Settembre
Pizza con Fichi e Prosciutto
Roll out pizza dough to fit a small pan. Top with olive oil and fennel seed. Layer with thinly sliced figs and bake for 20 minutes at 400 F. Top with julienned prosciutto and bake for another few minutes until crispy.

5 Settembre
Il Pranzo a Mia Casa
Slice figs thin and wrap with *prosciutto di Parma*.

Slice cucumbers and add salt. Toss with white wine vinegar.

Sauté garlic in ¼ cup olive oil. Remove garlic and add 5 minced anchovy filets, taking the pot off of the heat as they dissolve. Once dissolved, add a can of chopped Italian tomatoes; simmer for 20 minutes. Serve with cooked *orrechiete* pasta.

7 Settembre
Crustacean and Cephalopod Heaven!
Dust little octopi in flour; fry.

Sauté onion in butter, then add rice. Cook until rice becomes translucent. Add broth and chopped parsley to taste. Cook in 350 F oven for approximately 20 minutes, or until rice is done. Press rice into desire shape on plate. Arrange fried octopi atop rice and garnish with lemon wedges.

Broil skewers of shrimp, calamari and octopus brushed with a little olive oil. Serve along with rice.

15 Settembre
Pollo con Marsala
Pound slices of chicken thin. Turn in flour and sauté in butter. When chicken is cooked, add Marsala wine and cover until absorbed. Turn chicken to coat and top with thin slices of *fontina* cheese. Cover for a moment to let the cheese melt on top, then serve.

26 Settembre
Fiori di Zucca Fritti
Clean zucchini flowers and stuff each with one anchovy filet and a slice of buffalo mozzarella. Roll flower in a mixture of flour and water, then fry in oil.

27 Settembre
Rice Pilaf with *Moscardini* in Tomato Sauce
Boil, peel and seed 5 tomatoes. Boil an octopus or calamari head in water.

Sauté onions in butter, then add rice. Add a little white wine. Add the seafood head water (discard head), then bake in the oven at 350 F for approximately 20 minutes, or until done.

Sauté chopped fresh calamari rings with butter, onion, and peeled/seeded tomato. As the sauce begins to thicken, add chopped basil and marjoram.

Transfer the cooked rice into a donut mold, then turn the mold over onto a plate. Fill the space in the middle of the donut with the sautéed tomatoes and calamari.

1 Ottobre
Pappardelle con Funghi
Cut diced marjoram and basil into a small amount of soft butter.

Sauté sliced onion in butter. Add sliced porcini mushrooms and salt; sauté until they give up most of their water. Serve over *pappardelle*, mixing in the herb butter.

Top with Parmesan cheese.

3 Ottobre
Smoked Salmon Pasta
Julienne smoked salmon and fry in butter. Add vodka until it bubbles away. Add cream. Cover and cook for about 5 minutes. Serve sauce over cooked *farfalle* pasta.

Appendix: Images

Plate 1: Civita from the bridge at sunset

Plate 2: Tony's pergola

Plate 3: Statue dedicated to Civita di Bagnoregio and sister cities

Plate 4: Mother and baby donkey in open pen along the road to Civita

Plate 5: Luca de Troia petting his koi fish in the pond at Hortus Unicorni

Plate 6: Corner of the Marchesa's *palazzo* on Piazza Colesanti (the daylight shining through windows indicates where the structure fell away due to erosion and landslides; the rest of the buildings remain habitable)

Plate 7: Tony's *giardino* and the rooftops of his home

Plate 8: *Casa di Famiglia Rocchi* (Alessandra's parents' home)

Plate 9: My favorite icon in Bagnoregio, located at the corner of Corso Mazzini and Via Brunelli

Plate 10: Grave of Astra Zarina in Bagnoregio

Plate 11: Flowers for the baptism of Elena, granddaughter to Rossana and Antonio

Plate 12: Taken from Civita looking down into the valley during the onset of a storm

Plate 13: Civita's back road leading to the tunnel

Plate 14: Walking home with groceries up the bridge to Civita

Plate 15: *Amici*: Peppi, Josè, me, Gaia, Bernardo, Marcella, Tony, Marco, Inga, Maria, Ilaria

Plate 16: View from the Grand Canal in Venezia

Plate 17: Iole cafeside for spritz after our second day at the Biennale

Plate 18: Canal at sunset

Plate 19: Jerry Satterlee walking through Antonio's gate

Plate 20: Steps to Il Nuovo, my home in Civita

Plate 21: *La Bruschetteria di Famiglia Rocchi*

GABRIELA DENISE FRANK is a Seattle storyteller and urban food enthusiast. In 2010, she became a Fellow of the Northwest Institute for Architecture and Urban Studies in Italy (NIAUSI), receiving a two-month fellowship to write a book about her experience in the unique Italian hilltown of Civita di Bagnoregio. Gabriela continues to share her exploration of the world and its shared tables through her blog, *civitaveritas.wordpress.com*.